progressive elements in the Church  ...

banner) and the more conservative ...ers

and the Holy See) who expect me to support their agenda? Sometimes

this tension causes me not to state what I really think.

v) To come at it another way, do I refuse to let the Lord

come in all the way ↑ because I am afraid he will insist

on certain things (in terms of my personal life) that I am

reluctant or too unwilling to do or give up?

 eg. I like nice things, like good clothes, expensive

cufflinks, art objects, etc., etc. While most of these things

are given to me, I am very attached to them.

  Twelve years ago, I gave away all the money

I had and said I would never again have a

~~little~~ savings account or stocks, that I would keep only

what was needed to maintain my checking acc't, I

now have a savings account again. Even though

I deposit almost all my honoraria in a special account

of the Archdiocese which is used for various purposes,; even

though I give away a substantial portion of my personal

funds each year, in the last year or two I have been

given so many gifts that I now have a savings

account again on the pretext that I may need

it for mother, or myself later on. I need to take

a look at this again and decide how much

I should keep in savings.

2003

Merry Little Christmas

to my love,

your Joanne

DATE DUE
Fecha Para Retornar

10-3-10			
12/21/14			
4/1/15			

CARDINAL
BERNARDIN'S
STATIONS OF THE CROSS

CARDINAL BERNARDIN'S STATIONS OF THE CROSS

TRANSFORMING OUR GRIEF AND LOSS INTO NEW LIFE

Eugene Kennedy

Illustrations by
Ronald Bailey

St. Martin's Press ✹ New York

www.stmartins.com

Library of Congress Cataloging-in-Publication Data

Kennedy, Eugene C.
    Cardinal Bernardin's Stations of the Cross : transforming our grief and loss into new life / Eugene Kennedy.—1st ed.
        p. cm.
    ISBN 0-312-24645-5
    1. Bernardin, Joseph Louis, 1928—Death and burial. 2. Bernardin, Joseph Louis, 1928—Meditations. 3. Stations of the Cross. I. Title.

BX4705.B38193 2003
282'.092—dc21
[B]

                                                    2003041398

First Edition: August 2003

10 9 8 7 6 5 4 3 2 1

For
Anne Finucane and Mike Barnicle
Friends of Joseph

CONTENTS

FOREWORD

These meditations engage us with a man who achieved greatness but is remembered for his goodness. Joseph L. Bernardin, child of the Depression, was reared in a South Carolina county in which the Catholics were not hard to count and in the fine crosshairs of Klansman perception were indistinguishable from African Americans. Weren't these Catholics plotting to overturn our old-time ways and rule the country with their mumbo jumbo and their fruit stand peddler of a pope in the White House? Joseph Bernardin was the son of first-generation immigrants from a town on the icy breast of the Dolomite mountains of northern Italy. He came to America where his father, a master of the art, could coax sheets and blocks of marble out of the Carolina quarries. The young stonemason died when Joseph Bernardin was six and his sister Elaine just four and, as hard times brought their bitter seasoning to America, their mother Maria drew upon her own art as a seamstress to keep them clothed, fed, and educated.

An American story if ever we heard one, we say, a *Reader's Digest* tale of triumph over adversity in which the widow lives to see her daughter's children flourish and her Cardinal son's face appear on the cover of *Time* magazine. All this is true except that against the fixed expectations of American culture there is no happy ending.

Instead, the hero son, drawing on his combined inheritance of arts, is hailed for his gift of beguiling consensus out of conflicted bishops and stitching their words together on such subjects as the morality of Nuclear War so that they can survive the strains of the lengthy public debates about them in both America and Europe. Then, at the very height of his accomplishments, when many judge that he could well become the first American Pope, he is stricken with a cancer that kills him within fourteen months, leaving his work unfinished and at the mercy of new ecclesiastical leaders who prefer to leave it that way.

Americans do not like stories that end with the hero's dying and his life's work left untended if not overturned. They have little taste for such tragedy except as a bittersweet and easily reversible staple in soap operas and Larry King interviews. Optimist and Booster clubs, Rotarians and Masons thrived on the bare backlit stage of Bernardin's growing-up years, symbols of the pragmatic American ethos mistaken for the Spirit in popular religion in which success is virtue and failure is its opposite.

But tragedy lies at the heart of Christianity, in which, beneath the battered scaffoldings of the centuries, the Catholic Church has served the world better as a keeper of Mystery than as mistress and midwife of power. Jesus met a tragic end, his work inchoate at best, his closest followers dispirited and in disarray, a Mystery indeed that out of loss and defeat renewed life and a victory over death should arise.

This sense of the tragic as an element of religious experience invests our premise that the course of Joseph Bernardin's life reprises the Stations of the Cross, opening for us a vision, in the lightning of suffering and loss that strikes around us every day, of the same simple constant of religious Mystery. We contemplate in Cardinal Bernardin's life the suffering that comes always by surprise, the everyday pain that is of the same warp and weave as that of Calvary, the Mystery that identifies us, better than a paleontologist's inventory of our bones, as members of the same extended human family.

Joseph Bernardin's life tells us what happens when a man accepts the destiny that is given to few on behalf of us who are the many, to recreate the central motif of Christian spirituality—life, death, and resurrection—before our eyes. This challenges the American preference for undemanding mysteries, such as those of the once thriving New Age religions in which facsimiles of mystery—crystals, invisible fields of energy, and crop circles—look sacred through the tinted windows of the world-as-it-isn't.

These meditations arise from my own thoughts about the man who was my friend for thirty years and of how he entered and lived this Mystery, yielded himself to it, really, so that his life, especially in its final three-year parallel to the three-year public life of Jesus, reflected the most fundamental theme of the faith he practiced and preached of living fully, accepting death, and finding and giving new life in resurrection. He reveals the essentials of the Gospel life, this holy man for our time and, as I observe later, for our own long, current, unended season of loss, the mystery that seems to go against our American grain but runs deep in the heart of its wood.

To examine and reflect with a proper grounding in what really happened in the passion and death of Jesus, I have drawn on the work of another old friend, the late Father Raymond Brown, one of America's greatest yet most unassuming scripture scholars. His masterwork, *The Death of The Messiah, A Commentary on The Passion Narratives in The Four Gospels,* was published as part of the Anchor Bible Reference Library by Doubleday in 1994.

As he was in life, Father Brown remains an admirable companion and a peerless teacher as he accompanies us from Pilate's stone judgment seat to the rocky skull-like formation of Calvary, allowing us to peer through the sepia screens of two thousand years to see what really took place on those days of the week we now call Holy. As one does with the dead, I spoke often with him as I wrote these pages and just as often heard his voice drawing my attention to something I had missed or needed to phrase in another way.

I also talked often with Joseph Bernardin, whose presence may be felt by the unhurried reader in the way I continue to feel it in my life. Some, I know, will say that this is invention, imagery forming from sites in my central nervous system where clusters the electric residue of long ago events. There can be no argument on such matters and I offer none. For the issue is not what I remember but what Joseph Bernardin did in his lifetime and does in ours. Listen to him, watch him, and you may be surprised to hear how simply but clearly he speaks of the mystery of all existence to each one of us.

Eugene Cullen Kennedy
January 13, 2003

PREFACE:
A Song of Faith for
Our Season of Loss

The Great Mystery of the World as It Is

We entered a new but ancient place together on September 11, 2001. Our kin dwelt here long ago and left signals of their presence—burnt out hearths where they gathered as families, still vivid wall paintings of their daily lives and dreams, withered flowers laid tenderly on the biers of their dead. It feels as if we have been here before ourselves.

This is the Cave of Life on the East of Eden. Here, all our experiences, even those some think they discovered in our time, have all been felt before—love's deepest passion, middle age regret, the wonder of new life and old stars. Just beyond this everyday space there is a great aula in which our forebears stored their sorrow that we enter now to store our own. Unlike nuclear fuel that spends itself slowly over the centuries, human sadness never decays and sets ablaze the tinder of any cheap grace touched to it, of closure or counseling or New Age magic.

We have entered the great Mystery of the World as It Is, in whose luminous but cracked stained glass our sadness is but one panel. This is the religious mystery that, named or not, everybody knows, this Chinese box of mystery, this mirrored palace in which, losing ourselves, we find ourselves, and we are made prey by loving to time's penalties of separation and loss. On 9/11, the protective shutters of this world were wrenched away and suddenly we could see the broken, wonderful World as It Is, this place just right for humans, by the fiery light of the event that has made mystics of us all.

In a world that savors the new, an old devotion responds to our long autumn of mourning. The Stations of the Cross commemorate Jesus' last journey across Jerusalem to Calvary, the Place of the Skull, where he would die on a cross, "not thinking his kingship something to cling to," as Paul writes, "but emptying himself, taking on the form of a slave," finding the fullness of his calling by embracing the same mystery of loss whose ashen taste lingers in the cup that we are still passing on, hand to hand, along a line, broken itself here and there, that trails back over the earth's swell into night.

Since September 11, we have all been making this *Via Crucis,* but with renamed and relocated stations, or places of commemoration. Now we pause at dank and blasted subway stations, over the flowers on a thousand makeshift altars, at sidewalks streaked with candle wax and walls crowded with pictures of the missing; listen and hear Rachel's grieving, *Have you seen our daughter? Have you seen my wife? Have you seen our son?*

For months, a scorched steel cross juts out of the Calvary of the smoking ruins, our Place of the Skull, where, as at Golgotha, amidst waiting families mothers long to cradle their lost sons and daughters in their arms again. We reach the final station, Ground Zero, now the fresh tomb cut in the rock in which we find the body of Jesus, and the bodies of all the dead, wrapped as tenderly as his, and borne out of the rubble in hushed liturgies of loss.

 SEPARATION AND LOSS/ TIME AND ETERNITY

This country of abundance has been plunged into the mystery of loss that changes us all. What, ask commentators not wise in the ways of the World as It Is, should religion do for us now? What answer can religion give to the solemn question of the moment? Some put it to God Himself, *How, if you are a loving Father, could You allow this to happen?* Let God be God, others insist, what we want is meaning: what *meaning* can religion find in our loss? Religion, however, does not answer questions but prompts us to ask deeper ones. Nor does religion tell us the meaning of our lives or of our deeds or who we are. That is our work.

Religion does not solve mystery as much as it opens us to the *Mysterium Tremendum et Fascinans,* the mystery beyond measure that holds us fast, the mystery that is also our destiny: that of experiencing rather than missing, guarding ourselves from, or fighting off, the imperfect glory of life itself. For the mirrors in its palace have two sides and we must acknowledge the image in both if we are to see ourselves whole. There is no defense against Life as It Is, no insurance to buy, nobody to sue when its course displeases us. And we feel alive only when we accept Love as It

Is, embedded with every possibility of loss, leaving us ever at risk. God is not on trial in our lives, we are.

The Stations of the Cross recreate a universe of loss parallel to our own. Consigned to musty wall space in most churches and neglected, except in the interval of Lent, they speak freshly to our season of loss. They track the mystery of loss that finally overtakes Jesus to dissolve his work, his burgeoning movement, and his own physical existence, this *Mysterium Tremendum et Fascinans*, this loss that completes rather than destroys his life. This longstanding devotion, part pilgrimage and part prayer, steeps those who make it in this mystery that is seeded by another commonplace mystery, that of time itself.

This journey of prayer and remembrance, rooted in times lost and gone, retains its grace, transcending time by bearing that scarred chalice, that Grail of the Sacrament of all our human loss and sorrow. These meditations reflect incidents in the last hours of Christ's life but they symbolize the incidents in our own human book of days. They attune us to the eternal whose pangs we feel in time, in the plangent longing of Spring, in the yearning that is the lining of our separations, in hungering to lose ourselves in those we love, in our doomed wish to capture the quicksilver beauty of passing days, and in our ache to hold on to each other just as we are in this world just as it is, in this now that, named, is no more.

The experience of the *Via Crucis* cannot therefore be calculated or valued in any measurements of time. We are too deep into this Great Mystery of the World as It Is to scamper after the scraps of time that Church officials, mystified by real Mystery, attach as indulgences to certain prayers and actions. Such notions of commuting our sentences in Purgatory, a mystery in itself, by thirty days or seven years, or by a full pardon from the governor's house at midnight, are unworthy of this Mystery that involves us in time and eternity. Indulgences distract us from the Mystery, for they are deals made in the language of time that is not spoken in eternity. For time is less measurement than mystery and is ever related to sorrow and loss.

Cardinal Bernardin

Cardinal Joseph Bernardin embraced the Mystery of The World as It Is even before he became the archbishop of Chicago in 1982. He served for fourteen years in that office, reproducing these fourteen Stations of the Cross in his own life, from false accusation, to mockery by the high priests, to a long, exhausting public passage through illness to a Calvary where he died before the whole waiting city. Embracing the Mystery, he learned that his calling was not only to achieve greatly and to suffer loss, not only to take on high office, but to assume the low state of a servant and the transcendent life of a saint.

If Death became his friend, Loss became his daily companion—loss of his mobility and of his privacy; loss of his voice in Church affairs; loss, out of due time, of the world and work he loved—and loss now sits next to us or just across the aisle, too. For the Mystery of Loss, this central panel in the great but fissured window of the World as It Is, is well known to each of us. In this lambent setting, we see how extensive our losses can be in the World as It Is. Some are great and easy to identify, such as those of love or illness. Others may be small but they are just as real and they all draw blood. Loss visits us in minor misunderstandings, messages unreturned, letters that don't arrive, good jobs that go unpraised, and good deeds that go unrequited. Some are tiny but their bites are true, while other blows are smaller still and register only as their iron filings cluster together in a hum almost beyond hearing on our inner magnet for loss.

Joseph Bernardin experienced every manner of loss as he made this journey just ahead of us, not as Mother Teresa did on the streets where Death had the freedom of the city of Calcutta, but on those of Chicago where he had the love of his flock. We experienced it when Death forced its way on forged papers into the life-filled streets of New York, plunging us into this overwhelming season of loss, this Passion Play begun on September 11 in which we are the crowd, crying out before Pilate in one moment and weeping before the cross in the next and made numb now by loss beyond our comprehension. For this is the World as It Is and there is no escaping loss, and our only choice, as Joseph Bernardin understood, is to live it through.

 How Are We Redeemed?

This is not a *how-to* book nor a guide to perfect happiness and a hundred years of healthy living. It is about the Mystery in which we live, and in which, after September 11, 2001, we search ourselves to understand better what counts in life and how, as Cardinal Bernardin grasped, the best things we do—loving, working, creating—involve the constants of separation and loss. We meditate with Cardinal Bernardin on the themes of religious faith that we have heard preached about, all too often in language bracketed by time, that once seemed the business of another time or another galaxy, but turn out to be ever and always related to our everyday experience.

Theologians, we know, have explored and explained the life and work of Jesus for us for centuries. Preachers with flashing eyes and organ-swell voices do it this afternoon and this evening on television. They all seek to explain what we ourselves know in diluted ways in our own lives. Why do these Stations of the Cross exist at all? Why do they lead not to triumph but to loss? Why does Jesus take on our human condition and become our kin in loss, separation, and suffering?

Theologians and preachers seek formulas to explain this Mystery of Loss at the core of the Mystery of Redemption. They have offered, and we have often accepted, as willingly as children do the Catechism lesson, answers that, in the midst of our own great experience of Loss, may give us little comfort. Why did Jesus take on our human situation and did he have to suffer and die to redeem us from our sins? Amazing grace, yes, but did God the Father, as some tell us, demand *payment* for sin through the sacrifice of His Son?

We have grown up with the idea that *Christ paid for our sins* through his suffering and death. This bookkeeping metaphor— that Jesus offered himself as payment for our sins—is employed by scholars who speak of the *economy* of salvation. But can we imagine, or be satisfied within ourselves, that this Mystery of God's sending His Son into time can be explained to us in the vocabulary of accountants?

The Stations lead us to the Calvary that rises just beyond Ground Zero, a mount to which Cardinal Bernardin also made his way, station by painful station. And he asks in our name, not why God permits such things, but whether theologians who author such monetary appraisals of why Jesus lays down his life for us understand anything about why humans lay down their lives for each other. We must enter the Mystery of Everyday Redemption before we even approach the Mystery of Universal Redemption.

Meditating on the Stations of The Cross, we see that Cardinal Bernardin reproduced them in his own life. Do we recognize in our own lives these many stops just where the road divides and we face the same possibility of gain and the same risk of loss? Is it loss or gain when we find that the questions lead not to answers but to deeper questions?

Did God become man to pay off our sins, or to experience our sorrows?

 Sins or Sorrows

Which of these notions speaks to our human experience of the World as It Is? Is the suffering of Jesus a payment for our sins or a validation of our sorrows? Perhaps we may be ransomed from our sin but are we ever freed from our sorrows? The events of 9/11 force the question on us: Of which do we have a greater supply, sin or suffering? Which, from God, demands greater mercy, the human frailty that leads to sin or the human frailty that leaves us vulnerable to pain?

Can we be far off, in this lingering season of loss, in imagining that Jesus came at least as much to share our sorrow as to give his life in payment for our sins? Why is Jesus referred to as a *man of sorrows* if not because he looks on us as he did the multitude he fed on the mountainside, "with compassion"?

How can theologians miss what human beings can see clearly: that Jesus, and Jesus living in Cardinal Bernardin, beholds us not as men and women whose bills for sin must be paid but rather as men and women whose wounds must be healed? Jesus has an eye, we know, for the downtrodden and the discouraged, for those bound by paralysis or by pain, for the lame and the diseased, for men and women bearing their burdens of suffering and loss as communicants do the gifts of wine and bread to the altar where the Mystery of the Eucharist is offered.

There is no evidence that, despite inflamed preachers, Jesus ever looks at us or our world other than gently, cupping his hands around the guttering candle of our least efforts rather than snuffing it out. Unlike hellfire preachers or self-complacent high clergy, Jesus does not look on the human family to shame or humiliate its members for their sins. Sin, as Jesus often shows and as Joseph Bernardin knew as well, is easy to forgive. Forgiveness is already a seedling as we recognize the truth of our motives and actions and make our own the prayer that he urges as the simplest and holiest of all, the one perfectly matched to our condition: *Have mercy on me, for I am a sinner.*

 THE MYSTERY

If sin can be lifted away easily, suffering cannot. That is why even the weather sets off twinges in bones we thought healed long ago and why, spiritually, a few bars of music may instantly reinstate, at full strength, a sorrow that we thought had grown less with the passage of time.

What mystery is displayed hourly on television screens and newspaper front pages, that of sin or of the grinding and ubiquitous sorrow of the sick and the dying, the exiled and the afflicted, often bearing sadness and loss as all they have left of what they once owned. These are not great sinners in life but rather victims of ordinary living, clutching each other as they move along, ransoming their sorrow with love, sharing the last but finest treasure of human touch as the only thing that they can give each other.

Just over the horizon beyond them, anxious people wait in doctors' offices or sit restlessly outside surgical suites, and, beyond them, the legions of the bereaved place fresh flowers on new graves, and, just there where the road turns, men and women sit in wheelchairs, or pick at their meals in pale-walled nursing homes, calling in their old age for their mothers, yes, and there in the well lighted cottage, the young wife makes dinner for her children, her heart bearing a mean bequest of hurt from a deserting husband. We have been wrong, it is not the poor we have always with us, it is the suffering. Is this not what God sees better than we?

In this season of unfinished grief that symbolizes all that is unfinished or harshly interrupted or ended in human life, we can understand that the Mystery is different than we were taught, that sorrow far outweighs sin in this world. Jesus came, as Joseph Bernardin lived, not to pay for our sins but to minister to our sorrows. We enter the Mystery when we become wiser, through our suffering, than the theologians who insist that God became man to pay our bills so that we could lay down our sins. That is incidental to his first mission, that of helping us to bear the burdens of sorrow that we can never lay down.

INTRODUCTION:
Death Comes for
the Archbishop

The Cardinal and November are dying together in the dregs of the year's days in weather as hard and gray as the Chicago streets that are spread with darkness before dinner. The television towers poke their white crane necks above the century-old sentinel trees in front of the redbrick galleon of his residence. The deathwatch for Joseph Cardinal Bernardin has begun.

The hard city turns tender and holds its breath as its people seem to gather together at his bedside. Joseph Bernardin arrived as archbishop to some but he is departing as Cardinal of them all.

By its thief's habits, Death arrives in the night's bleakest passage to discover that no door is locked against his coming. The residence blooms with light that he might easily find the archbishop who has long since put away any fear of him. If Joseph

Bernardin is filled with easy light it has been hard-won through harsh trials of false accusations and ravaging illness. The archbishop's private prayer is to empty himself as Jesus had and not to cling to anything, and there is no darkness left in him.

Only after the death of Joseph, friend for thirty years, do I really see what I had for so long been watching close up. His journey is to be completed before any of us can grasp how modern is its form and how ancient its meaning. Joseph gives himself to building a post–Vatican II Church, but his own spiritual life is rooted in and nourished by its tradition.

Joseph dies on the fourteenth of November, 1996. He has been archbishop of Chicago for fourteen years. It is halfway through the fourteenth hour from the previous midnight when those who love him sense that his final agony has begun. His surgery for pancreatic cancer takes place in June, 1995 and Joseph speaks hopefully, like an innocent man reprieved, of being "cancer free." Fourteen months later the invader comes out of hiding.

The Stations of the Cross

There are fourteen stations in the traditional Catholic devotion known as the Stations of the Cross. Catholics carry it out by meditating on scenes from the climactic public afternoon of Jesus' life. They make a pilgrimage in miniature with Jesus through his last hours, from his condemnation and death in public to his body's being taken down from the cross and buried in private in the rock-hewn tomb.

This practice began with Christianity itself when believers, still concentrated in Jerusalem, could easily visit and pray at the actual sites of Christ's suffering and death. In the Middle Ages, a demand for depictions of these scenes arose from those in Europe, barred by fate and history from traveling to the Holy Land, who nonetheless wanted to make this meditative pilgrimage. This reflective journey recapitulates in itself the broader story of Catholic devotional life. Although these stations, once rendered in classic European oil paintings, have been reimagined many times in woodcarving, sculpture, and spare steel casting, the spiritual focus of this practice has never changed. Representations of these stations are to be found posted along the walls of Catholic churches and chapels throughout the world.

Accompanying Jesus on this path to Golgotha we find that our own experiences—misunderstandings, physical pain, rejections, feelings of being abandoned, and life's little deaths beyond counting—are spiritualized through their being melded with those of Jesus. We conclude the final station strengthened to bring our renewed faith out of the Church and back into our own lives. The stations are incomplete without this Christian impulse to reject spiritual complacency and to break through, to become unshelled, as the symbolic eggs of Easter remind us, and to respond to the pain and need of the world.

DEATH IS AT WORK IN ME, BUT LIFE IN YOU...

This conviction is neither one of revival tent emotion or of ordering another round of sentimentality. It invokes and symbolizes a basic Catholic belief about suffering as a meaningful rather than a random experience in human life. That was at the center of Joseph Cardinal Bernardin's spiritual life and remains the core of his heritage. Through his sacrificial life he fuses what is traditional in Catholicism with the post–Vatican II Church, realizing in eternity the mediator's role foreshadowed so clearly by his ministry in time.

All suffering, in this teaching, intermingles with that of Jesus and his work of redemption. By our gift of life we are implicated in redeeming the world's pain, in relieving by revealing the meaning of suffering. This conviction is integral to the Catholic ascetic life: that we participate through our own suffering in the work Jesus completed through his own suffering. St. Paul speaks of this Mystery—that is, a moveable feast of belief that matches our spiritual reach but ever exceeds its grasp—as our suffering making up for what was lacking in that of Jesus.

Paul explains this spiritual dynamic as he writes to early Christians that "Death is at work in me, but life in you." Even our ordinary suffering is made sacred as it is joined to that of Christ and passes, as Paul's did, as solace to others. So he claimed, as we can, too, that our losses may be counted as gain and our smallest deaths as fonts of life to others. Spiritual energy, like any energy, is never lost but only transformed to be passed on to others. That, in fact, is what religion is all about.

 # Hard Sayings

The popular culture shrinks back from demanding spiritual messages, preferring a kind of half-blessed passivity. A quarter of a century ago, largely because of the novel and movie *The Exorcist*, evil never burned inside men and women. It came from without, from the Devil as tempter and possessor of otherwise innocent souls. Nowadays our spiritual airspace is filled with angels, mostly of kindly deliverance, and we stand by waiting for their intercession.

Devils and angels—actors from spheres below and above who render us spiritually passive—rise and fall because they bob on a shallow sea of so-called religious conviction. Faith is never really dangerous in the New Age, mother of faux mystery and inert belief in which pseudoreligious experiences are delivered to docile followers. Such interpretations of religion curl like a burning page under the impact of the biblical injunction that it is "a terrible thing to fall into the hands of the Living God."

The Stations of the Cross abide because they encapsulate the central mystery of Christ's work of redemption less as a payment for our sin than a validation of human suffering through his joining himself to it. Those who profess to follow Jesus will encounter, in differing guises, the same experiences that he embraced on that first Good Friday. Believers in Jesus cannot profess a welfare faith in which grace is automatically deposited in their accounts on the first of every month. The massive central reality of the Christian spiritual life is the cross that, whatever its shape or nature, is not to be shunned but to be shouldered. It is a terrible thing to fall into the hands of the living God.

Some Catholics believe that Vatican II and its reforms removed this motif of suffering from Church belief and practice. They feel that much that was sacramentally profound about Catholicism has been rendered shallow as, for example, in the exchange of Gregorian chant for guitar masses. Sin seems, like a painting too stark for modern tastes, shifted to a remote and little-visited museum gallery. Softness in opinion and practice, in the judgment of traditionalists, characterizes the Church that has come into being since Vatican II.

Joseph Cardinal Bernardin is the model architect in the

United States of what Vatican II actually proposes, a return to one of the oldest ecclesial traditions, a collegial Church based on the college of the apostles formed by Jesus. He deplored the excesses that were bound, in such a massive change, to occur. But he preserved an uncompromising faith in the Catholic traditions that express the redemptive teachings of Christ. His true calling is recognized in his reliving the Stations of the Cross as testimony to the theme of Incarnation, Death, and Resurrection that flows through contemporary Catholicism from its headwaters in the ancient Church.

The Stations of the Cross provide a powerful symbol of the life that Joseph Bernardin led and the path that both traditional and post–Vatican II Catholics may walk together. This devotion, by which we make pilgrimage through Christ's last hours, has endured through the centuries because it not only recalls Christ's life but it also prophesies and reflects our own.

The Stations may lead us around the church but they always return us to the altar of sacrifice. The separation of Christ's body and blood is remembered in the separation of the Bread and Wine of the Eucharist. Such faith is indeed dangerous. If it promises ultimate triumph in resurrection, it also reveals that life in the spirit rises always and only from our active acceptance of death in its everyday hundred forms.

Nothing challenges more our popular culture—tempted as it is by anesthetics and half in love with euthanasia—than a religion that teaches that suffering can be redemptive rather than wasteful. How coarsely against the grain for a nation that idolizes the act of choosing more than what is chosen to contemplate the free surrender of choice that was at the heart of Christ's sufferings and remains the watermark dynamic of Christian spirituality.

If, hundreds of years ago, the common people asked for

symbols of these pauses on the *Via Dolorosa*, we, their counter-parts, have even greater need for them now. In an unparalleled spiritual irony, our preferred satisfactions have become like the hellfire described in old theological manuals. That flame torments the damned because it "burns but does not consume." Today's multiplied gratifications torment us because they consume but never satisfy us, they devour and leave us as we were: empty, waiting to be filled.

 CARDINAL BERNARDIN'S STATIONS

I can now calculate the cost of Joseph Bernardin's discipleship. He accepted in faith the calling whose price most of us shrink back from paying: to offer freely to the world a fresh representation of Jesus's life and death, to carry that cross from station to station to a Golgotha in the heart of our own life.

Joseph's own words reveal a soul striving to allow Jesus to enter and to take over his life and work. "I want desperately to open the door to let the Lord in so he can take over my life completely," he writes as he makes a private retreat a few years before his own death.

This longing of his soul increases at that "Turning Point," as he calls it, that occurs when he is archbishop of Cincinnati and, at age forty-six, president of the National Conference of Catholic Bishops and known throughout the world as a man on the rise in the Church. At dinner, a group of young priests ask him, "challenge me," as he describes it in his shadowed study a few weeks before his death, "to examine whether, under the press of other obligations, I am paying enough attention to my spiritual life."

From that day until almost his last, Joseph spends his first hour in prayer. How often, taking a cab to an early plane, I pass his residence before six A.M. and see the yellow light flooding through his windows into the darkness of a still sleeping neighborhood. How I long to see them again since I know now their signal of his work in progress, that of becoming a saint for our own time.

Joseph lives out an ancient death, the death of Jesus himself, to whom, knowing the risk, he makes every effort to give his life wholeheartedly. The risk, shunned by most of us, is—and remains—what happens when Jesus takes our prayers seriously. To Joseph, Jesus gives his own life and death to live again before our eyes—we, so like the crowds always just in the background of Gospel events, close enough to see and hear yet distant enough to avoid serious involvement. We can run any time we want to.

From the November afternoon in 1993 on which he is suddenly struck with a false accusation of sexually molesting a seminarian until the middle of that November night on which he dies, Joseph's prayers are answered in a way that confounds all of us. For Jesus makes passage through the gate of Joseph's soul to give him a three-year public life like his own.

During these three years Jesus brings the cup to Joseph who, having given himself wholly to the Lord, drinks it willingly. Joseph cannot immediately understand any better than we members of the ambivalent crowd that he is to make the stations and we are to follow him not knowing, until they are finished, what we have seen with our own eyes and heard with our own ears.

Joseph Louis Bernardin lived out the *Via Crucis* in a city that prefers to act tough rather than acknowledge its own beauty. But Chicago turns wordless as the mystery of Joseph's dying envelopes that leaf-shedding season halfway to Winter. We

18

watch but do not fully understand as Joseph, uncomplaining, accepts and carries his cross on streets never dreamt of as a *Via Dolorosa*. With him, in this city in the heart of America, we make that ancient journey into the mystery at the center of history itself.

The FIRST STATION:
Jesus Is Condemned to Death

Then

It is Spring and the days and the nights are equal.

In the heavens Brother Sun looks directly across the sky at Sister Moon and Passover is ushered onto the land swollen with yearning for new life. A few days before, Jesus is hailed as he passes through the city's great gate, and the hearts of the religious leaders also swell for they are seeded with uneasiness and distrust for this calm but unnerving man who makes such claims about himself in the temple sanctuary. They lay a word trap to snare him into blasphemy. Does this Jesus make himself greater than the law, shrugging off and standing clear of its tangle as he announces that, yes, he is the one who is coming, the Messiah the Jewish people long for?

See for yourself, *the leaders say, sweeping their robes back with their urgent gestures,* this Jesus rouses the people and threatens good order. *But these men have no authority in this Roman province of Judea to bring him to judgment. They must leach power from the Empire*—see how this man breaks your law and threatens good order—*and use Roman authority at secondhand to rid themselves of Jesus. The high priests have their own reasons; this man says that he is the Messiah, what more need anyone hear? They gather the silver pieces that the traitor Judas, wild-eyed and frantic, scatters at their feet, but not before his kiss singles Jesus out so that he is quickly seized. Even as they seal his doom they are fastidious to avoid their own. The silver touched by Judas is now signed with blood and cannot be redeposited in the sanctuary, so let us use it to buy a field in which to bury the poor, a potter's field, the field of blood.*

Jesus, who knows himself to be the Light, is taken in darkness softened by the Passover moon, the scuffle in the jolting torchlight so small and swift and near to soundless that, even as his disciples slip away, it leaves barely a mark on the memory of the night. Its milky veil suits the captors, with their swords and clubs, as they lead Jesus down from the Mount of Olives across the Kidron to the palace of the high priest: night and day, darkness and light, openness and shadows, they advance and retreat across the hours, overlapping here and sharply dividing there, a dance of the forces of life and death.

His captors bring him, bound, as John tells us, first to Annas for questioning and then to his son-in-law, Caiphas, the high priest that year, for trial. The scribes and elders gather and, toward dawn, the whole Sanhedrin, for yet another session before bringing him, judged worthy of death, to Pilate. Peter follows but at distance enough, sitting finally among the attendants around the charcoal fire they kindle in the open courtyard of the palace.

The religious leaders seek witnesses to swear, falsely if necessary, about Jesus' claims that he will destroy the temple and in three days raise it up again. But their testimony crackles with the electric fire of the lie and sears the air like the words that stream down like embers from Babel. Still, the high priest, knowing that a midnight trial is also theater, places his questions dramatically: What is it you teach and who are your followers? I have taught openly, *Jesus responds,* ask those who have heard me. *In the courtyard, Peter shakes his head for the first time:* No, I do not know him, I am not one of his followers.

The high priest presses his proof text question, Are you the Messiah, the Son of the Blessed? You say that I am, *Jesus responds calmly,* and I am. And you will see the Son of Man sitting on the right hand of the power and coming with the clouds of heaven. *The high priest tears at his garments:* We have no need of other witnesses, the sentence for such blasphemy is death. *The guards taunt Jesus, spitting on and striking him:* Prophesy for us, tell us who it is you are. *Then he is brought to Caiphas.*

The back-and-forth hours of jeering questions are washed away as the tide of night begins to recede. Before it runs out, however, Judas hangs himself from a tree and Peter, his face plain in the firelight, denies for the third time that he knows Jesus. At the first light of this Passover day, his captors hurry Jesus, bound and clothed in a robe of ridicule, to the Praetorium on the western heights of Jerusalem where Pilate rules in Rome's name.

Standing before it, the high priests reveal their infinitely practiced observance of the fine points of the law, for they cannot enter the Praetorium where Pilate sits or they will suffer ritual religious contamination. Does the procurator count these extra minutes a burden or a blessing as he walks back and forth from his questioning of Jesus inside his imperial walls to his wrangling with the high priests and the crowd gathered outside? He needs time, yes, more time, for he is in an uncomfortable position.

Pilate sends Jesus to Herod who is intrigued for this Jesus is said to work signs, Will you not work one for me before I send you back to the Roman authority? *Herod, who has manipulated many for far less, is not a man to lose face or pleasure in such a moment, and if he cannot coax a wonder out of Jesus, perhaps he may yet knead a favor out of Rome. Is this not a moment of opportunity that has little to do with Jesus, a chance on this morning to reach an understanding with the procurator that will serve us both well in the future? History embraces them for the unspoken deal they strike and we learn that they become friends from that day.*

Pilate has his own questions ready, for Rome has not sent a fool on this long dusty mission to keep order in this earth's-end province and he does not intend to stay here forever, put down this trouble and improve my relationship with Caiphas and the empire will reward me, I will not spend all my days here. *Yet this is no simple matter, for Pilate is made to straddle two worlds, that of the death demands made by those he governs and that of the good order he must maintain for Rome in whose name he governs. The high priests and the scribes and the gathering crowd want Pilate to execute their death sentence by the authority of the special stone judgment seat from which he presides.*

The whole crowd, the Gospel writers tell us, joins in the accusations that make Jesus a threat to Rome, We have found this man misleading our nation, both forbidding the giving of taxes to Caesar and saying that he is the Messiah king. If he were not doing bad we would not have handed him over to you.

Pilate goes back inside and summons Jesus to an exchange whose tension remains fresh. Are you the king of the Jews?

Of yourself do you ask this, *Jesus replies,* or have others told you this about me?

Pilate has his own question, Am I a Jew? Your nation and the chief priests have given you over to me. What have you done?

My kingdom is not of this world, *Jesus answers.* If my kingdom were of this world, my attendants would have struggled lest I be given over to them. But, as it is, my kingdom is not from here.

Then you are a king, *the procurator responds.*

You say that I am a king. The reason for which I have been born and for which I came into the world is that I may bear witness to the truth. Everyone who is of the truth hears my voice.

What is truth?

The question haunts us, in any language, at any time, on its own: What is truth, a question for ourselves as well as history. Do these few words bite because we may still hear, as Raymond Brown suggests, the imperiousness of Rome in them? Or is Pilate unknowingly and ironically bringing judgment on himself and the whole proceeding, confessing that he does not understand what Jesus is saying, that he, the Roman procurator, *does not hear his voice, does not understand his witness, is not himself of the truth. This is the last time Jesus speaks of the truth. For how many does Pilate ask his famous question? For now he will have Jesus scourged and release him if he can.* Look at him! *Pilate says to the crowd,* I find no case at all against him, *Pilate tells the crowd,* neither has Herod. *Perhaps he can find a way out for all of them.* By Passover custom, I, as governor, may release one prisoner of your choosing. Whom do you want me to release to you, Barabbas, the thief, or Jesus who is called Messiah? *Pilate knows that the chief priests give up Jesus only out of envy and jealous zeal, out of* phthonos, *that wide-spectrum word of violent dislike for the good. As they begin to stir up the crowd before him, he receives a message from his wife.* Let there be nothing between you and this just man, for I have suffered many things today in a dream because of him.

But the voices of the yelling crowd break his reverie, Barabbas, not this one but Barabbas. They make the choice that Peter will later describe as he preaches in the temple precincts. You denied the holy and just one, and asked that a man who was a killer be granted to you. *Pilate returns inside the Praetorium again, with another question,* Where are you from? *He is asking, Raymond Brown says, about Jesus as "God's Son," the charge that the procurator now realizes is the real one against Jesus, for who he is, not what he has done, is the crucial matter. Jesus does not answer him.* Do you not know, *Pilate continues,* that I have the power to release you and the power to crucify you?

You have no power at all, *Jesus replies,* except what was given to you from above. The one who gave me over to you has the greater sin. *For Jesus has already said,* I lay down my life . . . of my own accord. *Although they are inside, their voices can be heard by the restless and angry crowd. Pilate leads Jesus out before them—*Look at him!*—hoping to find a way to release him. The crowd yells contemp-*

tuously at the procurator, Fail to execute this man and you will be no friend of Caesar's.

It is the sixth hour as Pilate takes the seat of judgment, gestures toward Jesus. Look, your king!

But the people are roused, Crucify him, crucify him!

Pilate looks into their faces, Shall I crucify your king?

The chief priests turn the winch of pressure. We have no king but Caesar.

Does a sliver of his wife's dream stab at him, as his own sense of the innocence of Jesus does? He shrugs, nods to the attendant and the basin of water is brought in which he washes his hands of Jesus, of them, of the entire episode. I am innocent of the blood of this man, you must see to it. *He can hear the shouts*—Let the blood be upon us and our children!—*as he signals for the release of the bandit Barabbas, and gives the order, in Rome's name, that Jesus be handed over and crucified.* . . .

Now

Joseph has been judged publicly, even condemned to death, in many ways before that bitter cold middle of the night when time loosens its grasp on him and the darkness falls away and he is filled with God's light. Those of us who see him up close catch its flashes many times before we can give it a name. We finally recognize that the radiance we glimpse, like that of a door frame made luminous by the light beyond it, is that of holiness.

Some public misgiving and judgment, like the bite of an immigration inspector's stamp, leave vivid marks on his growing up years with his younger sister Elaine and his mother Maria: *Outsider, Italian, Poor,* and *Catholic* in heavily Protestant, Depression-ravaged Columbia, South Carolina. Those judgments are reinforced when they move into Public Housing for ten dry and hungry years. The Bernardins are bureaucratically cataloged, inspected as cards are by impassive gamblers, then shuffled and reshuffled in the cruel social poker of that time.

Judgment is in the air as Joseph puts aside the university scholarship he has won in order to pursue premed studies, and to enter the seminary instead. *Can you get it back,* the ever frugal Maria asks, *if you change your mind?* Joseph's seminary black suit is not a monochrome dreamcoat but, fashioned by his mother's hands, the garment is indeed a judgment on, as well as an advertisement of, the family's poverty. That Joseph and his sister Elaine never feel deprived of anything is the fruit of the family love that lies curled within the hard shell of Depression life.

Two kinds of judgment await Joseph in the culture of the priesthood that he enters just past midcentury. The first is made instantly by superiors who recognize his extraordinary talents and quickly heap responsibilities into his open arms. The other is made by some of his fellow priests who are ready to write him off at clerical discount.

These judgments track him throughout his life. The possibility of being misunderstood is imbedded in the increased responsibility he is given at each new assignment. The cynical clerics sheath their complaints in harsh wit. To them, Joseph is a once poor boy bound for ecclesiastical glory, a figure ambitious for power who nimbly avoids the slightest snares as he pursues the main chance. Nobody, they smirk, can be *that* skilled or *that* good without ulterior motives, what's he after anyhow?

A Greek chorus of critics move with Joseph at every level of his career, an assemblage as various and anonymous as the jeering mob that exhausts its false courage in lurching toward and then pulling back from Jesus. They question Joseph's presumption: what is the source of his judgment and whence his wisdom, too? Again, as with Jesus, some of the loudest condemnations come from jealous high priests.

Joseph is denounced with memorable meanness even after his death. The historian James Hitchcock constructs a theory without foundation, in a magazine article, that more people had waited in line to mourn previous Chicago cardinal archbishops than they had for Cardinal Bernardin. Or, in the faint praise judgment of his former colleague at the National Conference of Bishops, Russell Shaw, that, yes, he "was a decent man, the holiness must have come later." Years after his middle-of-the-night death in 1996, critics mass an offensive to blame him for the eruption of the sex abuse scandal among priests in 2002. This is a problem that he vainly fights to get his brother bishops to recognize and respond to in the early '80s. Yet, six years after he dies, a special Web site is devoted to this hateful posthumous judgment that Joseph is somehow responsible for the darkness on which he tries to shine the light. The light, that is what enrages men who love the cover of darkness, the light they do not comprehend. This boiling reaction of envy and jealousy within them is the same fouled bile of *phthonos*—the violent dislike for Jesus' goodness visited on him by the high priests— and their lies the same as those cascading in flames from the Babel of the witnesses at Jesus' night trial—reactions that spew from men in love with darkness, accusers who seem enraged by nothing so much as Joseph's goodness.

People biting on this same cud of envy dismiss Joseph's prayer life as external posturing rather than any true internal struggle in his own depths to achieve spiritual growth. These detractors find their marks and take their places randomly around the First Station, each accepting his destined role in the Passion Play of Joseph's life. But they fulfill his great destiny, too, as they embrace their own meager ones, donning the costumes of the high priests and elders who, finding nothing bad in the man, still cannot bear his goodness. Is he not the immigrant seamstress's son, can any good come out of South Carolina?

Their venom spouts like a knife wound in their calculated misunderstanding, the signature note on their cascading boos and catcalls, their stinging and shaming public accusations against Joseph's character and motives. If these attacks on Joseph run parallel to those on Jesus, Joseph does not think of that but of the cup of misunderstanding that is offered every day to uncounted and unnamed men and women.

If one of Joseph's cherished prayers is the petition of St. Francis "to understand rather than to be understood," it is a bewildering one when God answers it. Misunderstanding may also be the most common element in the Christian Mystery. All who take the message of Jesus seriously meet at the base of this First Station, this remembrance rock for everyone who has tasted the bitterness of misunderstanding or misinterpretation in everyday life. The shadow of this First Station falls on all of us.

We taste spiritual irony here as well, for few men have been more on guard against being misunderstood than Joseph. Does any other church leader do his research more carefully, craft his phrases with more awareness of their potential resonations, go to such pains to express himself more deftly—not a word more here, nor one less there—than Joseph?

To Work and to Teach could be his episcopal motto. These activities are fused in a transparent public life, I have spoken openly in the temple. That is his style as the traditional yet progressive leader of American Catholicism in the last quarter of the twentieth century. Within the Church he labors to implement the decrees of Vatican Council II, especially the return to the ancient "collegiality" that affirms the equality of bishops with the bishop of Rome himself, who is first among but not above them, and reinstates the process of bishops working together across the world and within their own countries to proclaim the Gospel in the light of the moral and social realities of the day.

Outside the Church, Joseph labors to his last day to justify the Church's raising its voice in the tumult of the Public Square. There, in a series of courageous and provocative addresses, he establishes the Church's relevance and its right to propose public policy guidelines on significant national issues, especially those in which human life is at risk. Dying on his feet, his voice cracking, his condemnation the watermark on his paper-frail features, Joseph makes this the theme of his last great public address at Georgetown University just weeks before he dies.

This consistent and fair-minded public Joseph Bernardin gradually earns the trust of his brother bishops, of his people and of thousands who only observed him from afar. This "credibility" is the modern version of *This man speaks as one having authority*. Rising swiftly in the Church, Joseph enters the Jerusalem of his life, under the waving palms and greetings of his brother bishops who choose him, before he turns forty-five, to be president of their National Conference. The cheers still sound in his ears as he is also named a permanent delegate to the Roman Synod of Bishops. They grow louder when, after becoming Archbishop of Chicago in July 1982, and a Cardinal five months later, his brown-eyed gaze from the cover of *Time* expresses his successful leadership of a bishops' committee that drafts the pastoral letter that, during the massive and popular arms buildup of the '80s, inspires, to the discomfort of the Reagan administration, a national meditation on the morality of nuclear weapons. Even some good Catholics in government suggest that he has roused the people against them, that he threatens the good order of the American empire.

Joseph also lives a private life, a hidden life, to be sure, in which he prays daily, and dangerously, that Jesus may take over his life so that, unafraid of criticism from any side, he will have the courage not only to preach Jesus but to live his life as well.

I want desperately to open the door to let the Lord in so he can take over my life completely.

As he hears within himself the anguished cries of ordinary people judged wrongly for their faith, their skin color, or their nationality, he comes to know their spiritual struggles too, for they are his own. For the pure and steadfast of heart, like Joseph, do this, mining in the darkness of their own depths, trying to throw light on themselves and their obstacles to union with the Lord.

Yet I seem unable to do so. I let him come in part way; I talk with him but I am afraid to let him take over. Why?

If his prayers draw him closer to God, the human conditions of his journey, with its doubt and wonder, bring him closer to average believers and the everyday faith that wrests peace and joy out of suffering. So, signing a quitclaim to a bishop's privileges, he enters ordinary time undefended, losing himself in the crowd but also finding and expressing there his full personal and pastoral identity.

He puts away the old man symbolically by losing the fifty pounds gained in the blurred universe of give-the-bishop-the-best-piece dinners, over which he gives invocations and benedictions beyond counting. Such banquets are black-tie judgments on religion's restricted entrance into the real world of men and events. Know your place, Bishop, be content with a portion of the fatted calf and your picture in the papers exchanging forced smiles with the governor.

Joseph grows lean, physically and spiritually, jettisoning extras and indulgences, getting to the bone of his destiny, building his long days of formal ceremonies and dedications on the simple early morning offering of himself in an hour of prayer and the celebration of the Eucharist, usually with Kenneth Velo or other priest living in his large residence. This Eucharist, as we see better now, draws him deep into its essential Mystery, that of the separation of the body and blood of Jesus, that sacrifice by which Jesus joins himself to all the human suffering of all time, that sacrifice by which he takes unto himself the death that seeks to take him, conquering it by embracing it. At each dawn, Joseph judges himself, weighing in the fine balance of his soul his own efforts to conform himself to Jesus, lowering his shoulder beneath the day's tasks, reducing, as a chemist purifies an element, what is left of his own want or will to make more room for the Lord.

Joseph, the mannered bishop, becomes a holy but not wild-eyed radical by breaking through the barriers, invisible but still as bright as crime-scene ribbons, that bar religious leaders from entering the conversation of the powerful and the influential. Know your place, Bishop, give the banquet blessing but do not try to change the water into wine.

But, as the Church teaches and Joseph knows, both Church and State share profound and overlapping interests in the conditions of their people's lives and work. And the Gospels are filled with tales of feasts at which Jesus speaks up or speaks out, a prophet keenly attuned to human suffering and need who makes the water blush into wine so that the wedding party might not fail, and makes men blanch at their own selfishness, too. Here, in these early hours as the rising light spreads acre by acre across the land, another light, at once kindly and fierce, illuminates the path that stretches before Joseph and splits here into a crossroad. By the light inside himself, Joseph makes a choice that is also a judgment. He selects the road that leads him to his life work and to his death, too.

For Joseph takes the dangerous path of spiritual growth that climbs steeply to Calvary. In the deep quiet of this private life, with the door closed against any neighbor's knowing, he offers himself in prayer to the Lord in that first and loneliest of hours before the world awakens. His prayers are wholehearted and therefore filled with peril. For if healthy ambition leads him to a Palm Sunday of shouted hosannas, earnest prayer and his entrance into the Jerusalem of the world also bring him to a Good Friday of suffering and death.

Joseph knows full well that he takes positions that will cause some to condemn him as a power seeker out for his own name and career in the marbled reaches of ecclesiastical influence. But he keeps silent, *I can only be myself,* Joseph replies when I ask him about this, *and do my work and let people learn what I am like and whether they can trust me. Trustworthiness is all that I have as a pastor.*

How easy to see now that it is precisely his trustworthiness that affronts his critics and motivates them to destroy him. If he can no longer be trusted, his influence in American Catholicism and national life will be shattered beyond any repair. Still, none of us is prepared—not Joseph, not his friends, not his people—for the fury of judgment that boils suddenly out of the everyday sea on that November afternoon in 1993. In this maelstrom of hasty judgment and false accusation, Joseph's three-year public ministry begins.

For here we encounter nothing less than a daylight attack on Joseph, a concerted and knowing effort to damage him spiritually. How dangerous he seems to a small band of editors, lawyers, and even a picaresque priest, Fiore by name, who with winks and whispers that give off the sour whiff of a shady merchant in Dickens, circulates highly critical stories of Joseph's life in Chicago.

Such madness, abetted by the unintentional but overconfident dismissal by diocesan officials in Cincinnati of the possibility of Joseph's being named in Steven Rubino's legal action, are currents of judgment that well out of the sea like a tidal wave on this afternoon. Fiore tries to associate himself in some way in this lawsuit soon to be filed on behalf of Steven Cook against Father Ellis Harsham for molesting him while he was a seminary student in Cincinnati. As October's days flutter down, Rubino, who has brought many cases against genuine clerical sex abusers, decides to bring Cardinal Bernardin's name into this accusation. Although his research is hurried, Rubino accepts an opinion from a woman, who later proclaims her lack of qualifications, that Cook has recovered a memory of Bernardin's summoning him to his bedroom several years before to perform fellatio on him. He makes contact with CNN, promising the news channel exclusive access to plaintiff Steven Cook if its editors are interested in covering the story. They accept the lawyer's claims and, two weeks before the case is to be filed, send reporter Bonnie Anderson to interview Steven Cook and to inspect on camera the evidence Rubino claims to possess that proves Bernardin's corrupted liaison with Cook. Evidence, yes, look for yourself how this hypocritical Bernardin can be seen in an exclusive photograph taken at the seminary with Cook, inspect the affectionate message in Bernardin's own hand on the oil painting that the prelate also gave him. Do not miss the compromising words of Bernardin's inscription on the flyleaf of the bible he presented to him, is this not the same middle-aged folly, the homosexual pursuit observed in Oscar Wilde's expensive wooing of his precious Bosie a century ago, what need have we of further witnesses?

As October collapses into the open grave of that November, the Archbishop of Cincinnati, Daniel Pilarczyk, enters this Passion Play. Pilarczyk is powerful, he feels that he knows just how to deal with these charges and with those who make them. Pilarczyk scoffs at Rubino's threat, approves an underling bureaucrat's letter of refusal, receives yet another warning in Rubino's renewed demand that Pilarczyk settle the case or he will file the suit, including Cardinal Bernardin, on the coming Friday.

Pilarczyk telephones Bernardin, *Rubino claims that his client has a recovered memory about you, about the whatever-it-is they say happened between you and Cook.* Joseph pulls back instinctively from this first shadow's falling, like the November darkness, across his life and work. Perhaps, he suggests, Pilarczyk should look into this, find out exactly what this nonsense is all about— a false charge could be very harmful.

He's bluffing, Pilarczyk retorts, *I understand these fellows, he'll never sue, this is all part of his strategy to get the archdiocese to settle, believe me, I know the type.* There was no getting through to him, Joseph says later, recalling his sudden sense of helplessness in dealing with Pilarczyk. *Can't you see that it's a bluff,* Pilarczyk sniffs, asking in his own voice a variant of a famous question, What is truth?

Pilarczyk admonishes Joseph not to be concerned, they wouldn't dare do this. He remained unmoved, complacent, washing his hands of the matter, let the blood fall on someone else's head, as, wittingly yet unwittingly, he offers Joseph to the crowd.

Within an hour the crowd roars back through the media, *Crucify him.* Before Joseph even sees the official complaint, the charges are broadcast around the world and he hears the shouts of the blood-hungry mob as he is offered to its judgment. An accidental sacrifice, as we now see, of the eternal bureaucrat raising his hands and turning away, destined to thwart history's judgment and seek its forgiveness forever, half a patron for all who plea that they know not what they do.

But this is only the first of Joseph's condemnations, as we shall see as we continue to make our way with him, perhaps at a distance as safe as Peter's from Jesus. A sentence of death is handed down not by a Pilate trying to stand, like the midday hour, halfway between the light and the darkness at the stone seat of Roman authority, but in the smooth, well-lighted place of medical authority as, with a heavy heart, his gentle physician, Warren Furey, delivers the verdict, *Pancreatic cancer, insidious, a year perhaps, this is the illness that will end your life.* Under this sentence from which there is no appeal, Joseph finishes the course of his life not knowing any more than we, the onlookers, that his garments are to taken away and his bones are to be numbered. But this is far into the Mystery of this passage, this Mystery, this sum of all things unfair that identifies Joseph's suffering not only with those of Jesus but with those of every man and woman of every age and place.

The Second Station:
Jesus Accepts His Cross

 Then

*The series of tableauxlike interrogations and judgments ends as the
first movements of a symphony do and one can barely take a breath
before Pilate turns away and the signature notes of the swift and
decisive final movement sound across this palace and courtyard where
Barabbas rubs his unchained wrists, and Peter stands stricken as Jesus
is yoked with his cross and led away by the same Roman soldiers who
witnessed his scourging and will now see his death. It is all swift
stumbling movement as Jesus "takes up," according to Mark and
Matthew, or "carries . . . by himself," according to John, the crossbeam, the* patibulum, *a word as smooth and weighty as the objects it
defines, a tongue of wood slotted in a groove to seal a door, or a
yardarm to bear a royal sail, each for a purpose as stout and unmis-*

takable as that of the crosspiece fitted to the neck of the condemned man. By custom, he will bear it along a crowded road, the better to advertise the shame and terror of this worst of ancient punishments, until he reaches the place where he will die. His arms will be nailed to this crossbar before it is fixed to the staticulum, or upright post that waits shadowless beneath the high noon sun (see Brown, Number 39, pp. 910–932).

The way of the cross begins with a ticlike convulsion of the crowd as it opens and closes again on Jesus and the soldiers. It signals neither riot nor uprising and a man keeping watch across the valley might pay it little attention and forget it until he is asked later, Have you heard, before it grew dark they crucified the prophet?

Now, as Jesus is led away by the imperial soldiers from Pilate's seat of Roman authority, he is followed by the people "and the women." The latter, Raymond Brown tells us, have a calling and a ritual to mourn a man's death before it occurs, striking their breasts as they tame its fierceness with their laments. Other Jews there are who also weep for Jesus for, like Pilate and Herod before him, they find no fault in him. Of these mourners, Brown tells us that "We are in the well-known context of the women who lament the dead by keening . . . (p. 920)." Still, this sound, encapsulating, as Jesus's suffering does, all the human suffering in history, cuts like a silver blade through the shouts and shuffling of the crowd as Jesus, given over to others as he takes his first steps along this path, gives in most of the Gospel accounts, the "impression that he is being led outside the walls."

Yet John tells us that the "place where he was crucified was near the city" and the writer Plautus that it was "outside the gate." But Melito of Sardis, another traveler through that same distant and dusty time, records that he visited the place and that Jesus "died in the city (pp. 935–940)." Does it matter, except to scholars, who, like mechanics enthralled by the engines but unmoved by the mystery of *flight, take their dry pleasures in plotting such details? Or is there, to this day, a symbolic meaning to this location that speaks to our depths as the themes of light and dark do? Yes, and the women, too, for they speak to us when the men hold back, crying to us across history as they accompany Jesus to the place of his death.*

 # Now

. . . It is the "letting myself go" that is related to Jesus' "emptying himself."

The way from here leads straight to death. Joseph will die in the city and outside of it, too, for he becomes the good shepherd to the whole country. The crossbar forced on him will finally be a cane on which he will balance himself beneath the cross that is no less real in its burden or bite because it is invisible to us. It is not lowered but dropped on his back, like cargo breaking free of its crane to explode on the deck below; there is no help for this now. Joseph's death will come from cancer but he will make his way to it in the aura of pain that clusters around this yardarm so rightly named for his voyage into the deep; yes, this crossbar, like those Jesus pulls loose from the thousand doors of the Kingdom that is falsely sealed by men who think to control the entryway by their petty regulations.

Joseph is about his Father's business, preaching of a kingdom whose doors open not to complex formulas or rituals but to the words that grow as naturally as Spring buds in the pure of heart. Joseph seizes and pulls free the bars shoved into place by those who would keep the Kingdom exclusive, drawing down curses onto himself for preaching that religion, pure and undefiled, that concerns our loving God by loving each other and is never found in the minutiae-swollen baggage that high priests pile onto the shoulders of men and women already bent low under their everyday burdens.

Joseph disturbs the high priests of American Catholicism, the other cardinals who look on America as Pilate did on Judea, a land and a people whom they control by their connection to Roman authority. These American princes of the Church are good men who are concerned about the Church but also about who is a friend to whom, and which of them can ask a question or send a report that will cause a head to nod in agreement in the heart of Rome itself? These men already hold great power as Joseph enters the last three years of his life.

Some of these cardinal-archbishops judge that Joseph remains too committed to the Vatican II Church to please them as they carry out the Pope's orders that hierarchical structures be restored in the Church across the world. Still, Joseph gives no cause for serious criticism in what he writes or in what he says. And he is thought well of by the people whom he recognizes, according to Vatican Council II, as constituting, in themselves, the Church. Those who criticize him seek out ways to snare Joseph in his speech.

They raise their hands and their voices in mock horror that he seems to understand, if not approve, the way some agencies sponsor campaigns to encourage the use of condoms to control the spread of the new plague of AIDS. They cluck like black-shawled Roman women exchanging gossip on the town square that Joseph seems openly sympathetic to homosexuals and that he has not, as they have almost to a man, followed Rome's subtle pressure to withdraw permission for the use of Catholic Church facilities for meetings of Dignity, an organization of homosexual Catholics who want to practice their faith and receive its support. This move is made casually, not by decree but by passing the word from one bishop to another; if you know what is good for you, you will withhold permissions for Dignity to meet in churches. And the map lights up almost overnight, almost all the precincts are heard from, except, of course, Chicago, and places like Seattle, where Archbishop Raymond Hunthausen feels that gays need the support of their Church and allows them to continue meeting on his cathedral property. The high priests cannot strike directly at Joseph but they can and do find reasons to question Hunthausen. After they ask for a Vatican investigation that will lead to his public shaming and virtual removal from office in the mid '80s, Joseph leads a movement to reexamine the issues and to restore his authority. What further need have we of witnesses?

Yet these same men finger their robes, avert their eyes, and remain silent as Joseph, during the same period, urges his fellow bishops to recognize, admit, and respond with understanding to the reports of a then-burgeoning problem of the sexual abuse of children by Catholic priests. There is no such problem, many Church leaders assert, what need have we of studies, programs, or, of all things, a national policy for a problem that is no worse in Catholicism than anywhere else? This Bernardin is very soft on anything connected with sexuality. That, the newly powerful among American bishops believe, is the real problem—that such bishops have used Vatican II to weaken traditional strict Catholic teaching on sex. Let this so-called sex abuse problem be handled, such as it is, by the lawyers, yes, and the insurers— case by case, diocese by diocese.

Joseph knows full well that other American cardinals speak subtle criticisms of him in Rome. Who is better at this, amassing decisive power for himself in the American Church, than Bernard Law of Boston who, as Joseph acknowledges, aligns himself with the Pope's program to dilute the reforms of Vatican II and to restore the authoritarian hierarchical structure to the Church? Joseph does not believe in a countercampaign of subterfuge, *I can only do what I believe in openly and let my work speak for itself*.

So the accusations reported to Rome suggest that Joseph is a threat to the Church by these things he preaches in the public forecourt of the temple. Other high priests, including James Hickey of Washington, D.C., affect alarm when Joseph proposes his *Unified Ethic of Life* in a lecture at New York's Fordham University. Feeling that the Pro-Life position of the Church loses more than it gains when it is lighted as if it is the only candle to hold against the dark, Joseph links a series of related moral positions, ranging from capital punishment to infant nutrition, to the Church's central Pro-Life program of opposing abortion. Take life seriously and you must take everything about it seriously. Despite the distinctions Joseph makes, and the renewed dialogue he inspires on the issue in the culture in general, these leaders and others mock his position by distorting it, claiming that this folly, as they see it, weakens the Church's commitment to eliminate abortion.

Joseph prays during these days that he may empty himself of concerns about what his critics say about him, as in Paul's description of Jesus' emptying himself and not clinging to his Godhead so that he may better accomplish his work. Is it a surprise or an unmistakable sign that he is right when Joseph hears the shouting critics and feels the cross lowered onto his back? Joseph's back becomes the cross itself, splintering and flaking because of the onset of osteoporosis and made more porous still by the radiation treatments for his cancer, and, finally, by the development of stenosis that closes its grip on his ravaged spine a little more each day to send pain showering from the nerves within.

Joseph "picks up the cross," and "carries it himself," as he is yoked with a crossbar that is sewn directly into his bone and flesh and nerve. And yet there is revelation in this, even as there is in the women who follow Joseph. The revelation in this darkness comes from the light that Jesus' suffering, experienced now by Joseph, casts on all the suffering of all the centuries, on that we know about and on that hidden in places that have never been searched and graves that have never been opened. Joseph bears his share of our mystery, this mystery of mysteries, the suffering of all human beings, this vast network of pain running deep in the earth drenched in the blood of the innocent, our common inheritance of suffering that is more often cursed than named accurately, that is denied even though it is found in every life, that is deemed of no value because it is so randomly and senselessly inflicted, this suffering against which angry men shake their fists against God: how can He be a loving creator and let tragedy run riot in His creation?

Joseph knows that the Holocaust is an example of this vast suffering, this slaying of six million Jews in Nazi Germany that is only one chapter in the long history of anti-Semitism that has been fed at times by Catholic leaders blinded to its evil. Finally, at Vatican II, under the inspiration of the great Pope who convenes it, John XXIII, the Church faces its own responsibility to correct the wicked distortions that blame the Jewish people through every generation for being Christ killers, for rejecting, mocking, and crucifying God's son. The Church makes clear in that council that the Jewish people cannot be condemned and punished for the death of Jesus, that we must relieve the immense suffering of the Jews, planned with such calculation in so many empires, abetted by followers of Jesus who shrug their shoulders or stand by as if they could separate themselves from the mystery of suffering, the *Mysterium Tremendum et Fascinans* that Jesus now enters. At his cathedral wake, the rabbis of

Chicago will hold a service for their great friend who understood and took upon himself their suffering and their causes. In the three years of public life allotted to him after he is falsely accused of sexual abuse, he visits Israel to make a sign of his support for the people who, out of Christian misunderstandings of the death of Jesus, have drunk as few other people have of the cup of suffering.

Jesus here accepts the cross fashioned from all the pain of all the ages, identifying with it, affirming its profound human and heavenly significance as the great and central *Sacramentum Mundi*, the sacrament of the world as it is.

The THIRD STATION:
Jesus Falls the First Time

 Then

In Luke (23:25), Pilate gives Jesus over "to their will," to the will, Raymond Brown explains, of the chief priests, the rulers and the people, to their will, *words sung into the shimmering aftermath echo of Jesus' prayer in the garden of olives. For Jesus, sleepless, prays near his disciples, sleeping, in this grove where Judas kisses him, not* my will *but* your *will be done.*

We hear the rustle of the leaves in that garden of olives just before the night is turned back like a bed quilt by the torches of the soldiers and Jesus, kissed by Judas, stands vulnerable to the armed men who rush toward him. Jesus does not turn away but looks straight into their eyes. They hesitate, feeling fear as this defenseless man stands without fear before them, hang motionless for a moment, stumble backward and fall to the ground (John 18:6). Their retreat is not worked by a magic hard-won by Jesus in a duel with Satan, but by his own moral authority, the power of his light over darkness.

Here Jesus enters the headwater Mystery and the last act of his mission, knowing fully what he accepts wholly, that he is working out the will of his Father, that all the human actors—the soldiers and those who give them orders—are incidental, that no man can give him over to the will of those who are set against him because Jesus, of his own choice, accepts the cup given to him as his Father's will in this hour.

The high priests give him over to Pilate's judgment, that judgment that contains—as the first tree of Eden contained the seeds of every forest—the basic elements, as near to necessary as water and air for every man and woman, those mystery-ridden pairings that contrast with each other as sharply as dawn and sunset. Count among them truth and falsehood, light and darkness, good and evil, and do not forget those, curled together in the deepest recess of the Mystery, that seem to be one with each other, facets of the same never-to-be-cut precious stone that dazzles the jeweler's eye and our own—love and labor and suffering. Are we surprised that Jesus, shouldering the sufferings of all the centuries, should stumble beneath this burden and fall on the stone path that leads away from the stone seat of Roman authority toward the place of execution?

There is no mistake about who prods him along and who will nail him to the yardarm that, as he falls, falls upon him. The gentiles, not the Jews or the Jewish people in general, and not the Jewish people down and throughout history, hold him captive to their will as they move away from the Praetorium as haltingly as Jesus staggering beneath the crossbar. Pilate has made the choice that forever defines him in his encounter with Jesus, handing over faulted this man— Look at him!—in whom he finds no fault. He chooses against the truth and against the light.

Echoes envelop us as we watch the guards pull at Jesus, as federal marshals do as they muscle a famous prisoner through the crowds to a modern courtroom, it comes to the same thing; move along, out of the way there, stand back, all of you. Listen and hear the sentence that drifts back like smoke from an old encampment in the book of Leviticus (24:14): The blasphemer is to be taken outside the camp and stoned by the whole community. Against the noisy shuffle and sudden silences of the milling crowd, Jesus struggles to regain his balance beneath the crossbar and time itself turns molten and the wispy drift of our common memory recalls the stoning of Naboth outside the camp for cursing God (1 Kings 21:13) and to another stoning soon to happen, of Stephen, also dragged away from the city, to become the first martyr for singing of his glory (Acts 7:58).

# Now

Joseph falls many times on the way to his death. As many and more of these are hidden as those large and small stumbles that are seen in public. For Joseph's walk is different now that his back has become the crossbar that cannot be shifted or handed off to any man. Three years before, he is weighed down with enough to make any man fall, as, in a confused series of events, archdiocesan officials in Cincinnati make decisions that hand Joseph over to the will of the courts and that of the crowd, the man in whom they can find no fault: let the responsibility be on others, not us.

The cable channel CNN embraces Joseph in the flowered summer before that November in 1993 when his three-year public life begins. Knowing that he has done more than any other Catholic leader to name correctly and to deal openly with the problem of priests who sexually abuse children in their care, CNN producers request an interview for a documentary they are making on the subject. Joseph agrees, feeling that the words he speaks in this vast public temple of television can cast light on a scandal that many of the other high priest princes of the Church deny or want to leave deep in the darkness in a grown over and unmarked grave. *They shake their heads,* Joseph tells me once, *when I bring up priest sex abuse, they say they have never heard of the problem. . . .*

The CNN producers, camera crew, and interviewer arrive as

friends, giving Joseph a hearty embrace, here is the man, let us seize him in our own way, taking him and keeping him in the dark about the reasons for seeking him out. They will use the tape, with its sex and lies, with rating points as their pieces of silver in their Passover of the sweeps time of November, on the Sunday evening before the National Conference of Catholic Bishops opens its meeting in Washington, D.C. The embrace is linked to a revelation that unjustly marks Joseph for doom; Here is the man, seize him. But before that Joseph must be sent sprawling before the whole world.

CNN uses the tape, this record of Joseph speaking openly, to indict him as a hypocrite, to make him stand before the crowds—Look at him!—for the charges they have been working on for weeks, claiming that, when he was archbishop of Cincinnati, Joseph sexually abused seminarian Steven Cook. Tied to the interview will be the testimony of this Steven and a presentation of the alleged evidence—the pictures of Bernardin and Cook together, the oil painting autographed by the Archbishop, and the bible signed affectionately by Bernardin—make no mistake, for in our trap we find another middle-aged Oscar Wilde and his precious boy—that clinches the case and makes the guilty verdict certain, what need have we of other witnesses?

CNN is given exclusive access to Steven Cook by his lawyer, Steven Rubino, two weeks before the spurious charges against Joseph are to be made public in that November. CNN and Rubino become friends from that day. After the story about Joseph breaks that Friday, CNN begins running the teasing previews that herald their Sunday evening program on sex abuse in which the Cardinal's own interview will be used against him. The promotional spots show reporter Bonnie Anderson interviewing Steven Cook, purporting to show them examining the evidence of these gifts, how typical of a man of power to seed his seduction with pledges and presents, you can read it in the photograph of them together, and watch carefully now as Steven Cook gives tearful witness to Bernardin's abusing him sexually and then casting him aside. No, he could not at first remember but he has been visited with his equivalent of the dream of Pilate's wife. He holds a string tagged to a battered kite of memory that zigzags across the sky of his consciousness when a therapist hypnotizes him and he remembers, yes, the Archbishop called me to his bedroom . . .

Reporters of all kinds converge on Chicago because Bernardin has been betrayed less to the official authorities than to the media gods, the court of public opinion where rough justice is meted out swiftly in American life. And here, indeed, in the city whose motto, *urbs in horto*, boasts that it sits in a garden, the story is reenacted before our eyes. But it is blurred at first and it is only later, as the scales fall from our eyes, that we recognize where we are standing and what we are seeing.

Look here, within the archdiocesan offices that stand as bold on the east side of Chicago as the Praetorium does on the west side of Jerusalem, as the boisterous crowd seeking news gathers in high excitement. The city so rich in the knowledge of good and evil has had no comparable story since its own Barabbas, Al Capone, whom the people cheered as their champion in public places, had been imprisoned half a century and more before. The atmosphere is charged, the camera lights sway like torches as the reporters search Joseph's face for reactions. Joseph bids his assistant bishops and aides, the disciples and the loyal women, to keep back. He asks the lawyers and public relations experts to put up the swords with which they would hack off the listening ear of the media giant. Joseph chooses to stand alone—there will be no need for a fresh betrayer to identify him with a kiss—to face those who would take him under their will and prevent him from rising after being driven briefly to the ground by the body blows of the first attack on his goodness barely a day before.

But Joseph gazes gently into the eyes of the reporters, speaks softly as, without notes, he begins to answer their every question fully. Only a few moments before, he tells me on the phone that he is not going to use any legal maneuvering—*I cannot speak about a matter under litigation*—or public relations spin—*You will have to speak to my staff about that*—to defend himself. He prays instead in his office, not my will, but thy will be done. *I believe*, he tells me, *that the truth will make me free, I believe that and I am going to answer every question as fully as I can.*

As Jesus once said *Let the dead bury the dead* so now Joseph says, *Those that don't agree with this can go to hell.*

And the surging reporters quiet as Joseph speaks, his gentleness taming the room's wildness with a quality that they, their ears ringing with the Chicago Blues of deceitful pleas and shallow excuses from governors and gangsters, seldom hear. They lower their notebooks under their uplifted pens, what is this sound so rare in public discourse in the great city? What is this sound, quieting us, calming us, too, if it is not that of truth? They do not fall to the ground but they stand arrested in place, their lips parted, their heads canted in attention, unable to shake off the light that is scattering the darkness at noon.

They had hurried, sure that they would find a man already fallen under the weight of the charges fashioned secretly but made with a deviousness perfectly partnered with the long spread of the night hours so that Chicago, like Jerusalem, is inflamed by dawn. The crossbar had been fitted into place on the national and local news programs, and in the morning Joseph's face stares, as if from a WANTED poster, out of the newspaper boxes on every corner of Michigan Avenue: *Look at him!* Fiore, the accusing priest, is living in a Madison, Wisconsin, mansion and running his family's business as he fights his own eventual exit from the Dominican religious order, gives testimony against Joseph to anyone who will listen, *Yes, this is true, I have been watching him for years.* Only Bill Kurtis, on Chicago's CBS station, raises a hand of protest on the ten P.M. news; this may be part of an effort to disgrace the Cardinal made by a motley group of critics.

Still, Joseph feels the crushing weight of false accusation during that long Thursday night that has yielded now to Friday afternoon. If the pressure throws him to the ground during those hours in which rumors clog the airways like unsorted chaff—*Yes,* a supposed insider tells a radio station, *another Cardinal has arrived to force Bernardin to step down immediately*—Joseph rises by dawn determined to bear this cross into the world where, as he tells me, *Millions of people now know only one thing about me, that I am accused of sexually abusing a young man several years ago.*

Nobody can do for him what he must now do for himself. He is anxious, yes, he has spent the night in his rooms, calling his sister, Elaine, in South Carolina, to speak to her about the charges and about their mother, Maria, who is now living nearby, cared for by nuns, some days are good but more are bad, *What can we tell her, will she understand, how much does she already understand?* Joseph remains sleepless even as his closest priest assistants sleep fitfully in their own quarters in his large residence as quiet now as even the raw and restless streets of the city are at three A.M. Joseph has his wakeful night and his agony of prayer, rendered stark and simple by the harrowing circumstances, *Not my will but Thy will be done.*

At first light, and despite the many supportive calls he receives, Joseph rises from the long fall of this night, but the crosspiece remains in place. He feels its invisible weight as he thinks of the priests who live under the same roof with him, Father Kenneth Velo and Father Scott Donahue, they would do anything for him, as would the Felician nun, Sister Lucia, who runs the household, and the nuns and women who help her. Joseph knows that he can count on them, but he has also come to know others, like the Cincinnati officials, who find no guilt in him but hand him over accidentally to the crowd anyway. But the crossbar is on his shoulders, can the most loving and loyal of his friends feel its splintered heft as he does? The judgments are drawn against him, he must bear this cross, through the parting crowd of blurred faces, by himself.

Before he offers Mass that Friday morning, a letter is handed to him, retrieved from the tall front door of the residence, and it is from a man Joseph has counted as a friend, a man whose home he has visited, at whose table of hospitality he has sat. The letter is like a taunt from the crowd, a rude shove strong enough to make him stumble, *If I had known what kind of a man you are, I would never have allowed you into my house. . . .* Joseph feels this blow keenly, for the invective of this man, a friend no longer, takes his breath away, these words of unremitting judgment and rejection, this conclusion, as he says after reading it to me on the phone, that he is guilty as charged, crucify him.

He feels this and all the other bruises of this night during which, if he has had defenders, he has had those who cackle like fire-lit Shakespearean hags at the fate that is now embracing him with its Shivalike arms. He pulls himself up, his body bruised, his garments blackened by these humiliations, he listens to the wise men who come to his office under their own star, the lawyers and the public relations counselors laying down their treasure boxes of advice. They urge him to speak a language he does not know, these are passwords from the vault of darkness, *To put out their fire you must burn a fire line through the forest, here is the kindling and here the flint, set their world ablaze.* He understands their good intentions, their goodness, too, but they convince him not of their view but of his own. He cannot push aside the chalice from which he must drink, he cannot treat the event as the fighter does the bull, he must stand firmly at the center not flee to the side of the event, and he must stand alone for the interrogation. *Do you think, Your Eminence, that the truth will really make you free? What is truth?*

Joseph stands tall now, calm, self-possessed, recovered from the impact of the charges that sent him briefly sprawling before the whole world, that fall that has brought this itching crowd to see me for itself, to hear and make its judgment on my answers. And what is this he feels, as good people must feel when what they see and believe in is contradicted, derided, made to seem an illusion by the powerful who would make them exiles in their own homeland? Joseph feels the *otherness* that settles into the souls of people who seek the light when they stand before judges who love the darkness. How outside the spectacle they feel, as if they are watching their own lives from behind a heavy glass that swallows the sounds of their beating upon it.

How hard for Joseph, as for all good people, when they seem deliberately cut off from participating in their own destinies, how difficult to rise again and believe in the truth in the face of those who cannot stand their light and will not give them space, there is no room for you here, no place for you or this dangerous light you would bring into our complacent darkness. This is a passage everybody makes—parents and lovers and priests and artists, teachers and doctors and writers, everybody with a good question or a new idea, everybody bearing a unique light into the darkness that does not want to comprehend it.

And here, in this turbulent space, the darkness begins to recede. We watch a crowd gathering on the wild energy of the day to see what this man has to say. Joseph walks directly toward this crowd, it tears at the edge, gives way and Joseph passes through its unraveling shield unharmed. The crowd members are transformed, their hearts unclogged by the power of Joseph's goodness, they have no will to strike him—Why have we gathered in this place against this man?—they lower their weapons and their eyes, they cannot stand armed before this man who stands unarmed before them.

Afterward, a veteran reporter describes how the journalists enter a press conference and find themselves inside a mystery instead, and soon conclude that they find no cause in this man, indeed, that this man is just, that he is from God, that he is what he says that he is. But there is more here, for mystery may be poured out, but its level remains full in its vessel, and so the reporters find themselves changed, their hearts different now, at peace where they were frenzied moments before. *I wanted,* the old reporter says, *to go up and hug him and tell him, Don't worry, Cardinal, everything is going to be all right.*

But there is one last question from a young man who has missed the mood change; *Are you sexually active?* The rustle in the room breaks off, in the sudden silence the dragon's eye brightens again, who knows what may come as the waters quiver, will the tide shift and run against Joseph again? Joseph does not blink behind his oversize glasses. He looks gently at the young question, *I have always led a chaste and celibate life,* he says softly and the coin of chance that has been spun into the air lands face up and the afternoon is made whole again. Joseph stands clear of the place of his first fall, the doubting Thomas who probes his wounds doubts him no more, there is nobody in the room, nobody but the hardest of heart in the television audience who does not believe Joseph. The truth makes him free and frees the journalists as well.

The FOURTH STATION:
Jesus Meets His Mother

 Then

This greatest of all religious mysteries is not without mysteries of its own. If we now stand in the crowd spread along the harsh way to Golgotha we may wonder that we have not caught sight of Mary, the mother of Jesus, before this moment when their eyes join like flints that kindle a line of light between them through the high noon dimness. Yet Jesus must turn away as he once did from both Joseph and Mary to seem lost but to be found going about his Father's business among the wise men at temple. Now, in a move that bears all the pain of all the separations, by force or by choice, of all the generations, he turns back to finish that work in which he will again seem lost but will be found again.

There is no record in the Gospels of their encounter here. Their meeting lies in the memory of tradition and in the earliest religious practice of the Stations of the Cross. Where is Mary to be found if she is not huddled with the women who send shivers through us as they follow Jesus keening in anticipation of his death? Where is this woman about whom we feel we know so much only to find that we know so little?

The author of the fourth Gospel, John, finds her, just beyond this dusty and stifling midday hour, standing by the cross. Yet no other evangelist sees her there. John himself has not mentioned her since she urged her son to come to the aid of the wedding party embarrassed that the wine was running low at the celebration at Cana.

If Mary is hard to find in this milling and shifting crowd, she is not much more easily found anywhere in the other Gospel accounts. Matthew (1:18–25) tells us of the mystery of the conception of Jesus and Luke affirms it in his account of the angel's annunciation of Mary's calling (1:26–38), that is followed by his story of Mary's singing her Magnificat on her visit to Elizabeth (1:39–56). Luke also relates her giving birth to Jesus (2:1–20) and the ritual of her purification afterward (2:22–39). We catch glimpses of her in moments so familiar to us that we might swear that we were there as eyewitnesses—at the arrival of the Magi and as the little family gathers its few possessions and hurriedly takes flight for Egypt (Matthew 2). Later still, we see her at that crossroads split where the callings of mother and son first diverge as he slips away to confound the elders in the temple (Luke 2:41–52). And Luke, the physician who would take note of such things, tells us that Mary does not miss the significance of what is happening, that, like every mother who senses the future shaping itself in her children, she is stirred as she catches hints and glimpses of this son's destiny, and that she carries these visions in her heart and thinks deeply on them (Luke 2, 19:51).

The Gospels seem like so many family albums whose loose pages and torn-away pictures enhance the presence of those who seem miss-

ing, just to the side, out of view, or behind the photographer, the one at whom the group is smiling expectantly; come, sit with us, the picture is empty without you. After these accounts of early years, known as the Infancy Narratives by scholars, Mary may, like the mother just behind the picture taker, be present but is seldom seen in the album Gospels of Matthew, Mark, and Luke, those written closer to Jesus' life than that of John. He, the long-lived eyewitness, has time and memory out of which to fashion a drama as theologically powerful as it is historically correct.

We sense and sometimes glimpse Mary in the other Gospels, for, as with many mothers, everyone in Nazareth seems to know her (Matthew 13:55; Mark 6:3). She is present, as we shall see, when, instead of unscrolling a list of commandments and prohibitions, Jesus invokes human relationships to define membership in his kingdom. We read (Matthew 12:46–50; Mark 3:31–35; Luke 8:19–21) of a visit of Mary and the close kin of Jesus that he draws on to explain further how human relationships rather than strained abstractions define his kingdom. The one who does the will of the Father is as close to me as my nearest relations.

At Cana, Jesus takes the occasion of his mother's nudging him to be mindful of the needs of others, do this, will you, for me, *to sharpen the definition of himself as separate, begun as the lost boy in the temple and extended now, in the midst of a family reunion, in his laying down again the conditions for, and the meaning of, being in relationship to him. Against the noisy background of the wedding reception, Jesus, as Raymond Brown expresses it, "dissociates himself from her concerns, placing first the hour assigned to him by the Father (p. 1020)." And here, too, against the grain of the generations of writers who celebrate unbroken harmony between mother and son, Jesus introduces tension into their relationship. The unexpected ambiguity, draining all sentimentality from the scene, is also disconcerting. These coins ring as they are scattered in the marble sanctuary of his-*

tory, these heavy coins spinning unpredictably until, face up, they give fair but brutal measure of the human cost of this son's loving his mother no less even as he leaves her behind in order to carry out the work of his Father. She feels every coin of this final payment fall within her heart, and who pays the price, he or she, for this mystery, raising to a power beyond calculation the separation known to every mother and son, as Jesus pulls away from her to give himself to a different relationship?

Brown pauses as this station composes itself just beyond us, this meeting called up out of tradition, this coming together that is also a parting at the same fork in the road at which Jesus first took a step away from his mother so many years before. The moment is rich in implication and prophecy. "These are the only two Johannine passages in which the mother of Jesus appears," Brown tells us, matching Mary's expectation that her will would be done at the wedding banquet to her waiting by the cross for the Father's will to be fulfilled on Calvary. Here the headwaters Jesus has been seeking are loosed to overwhelm the dams of time and to feed the imaginative stream of this meeting, making it inevitable, for who can deny that the eyes of mother and son find each other at least once above the bobbing helmets and between the raised and flailing pikes of the Roman guards?

As the jostling crowd opens and closes itself, allowing mother and son fleeting mirror fragment glimpses of each other's face, we listen again as Father Brown anticipates the last scene on Calvary that confers moral unity on these moments of choice and makes their relationship "to that of Cana clear." Mystery is invested inside mystery at that feast and at this offering for, in each place, Jesus addresses Mary as "Woman." This is "an address perfectly proper for a man to a woman, but never for a son to his mother," except in this context in which its use accents what Jesus himself emphasizes, the new relationship to him is not automatically granted on the basis of blood but flows first from faith in him, from believing in him.

This is amplified when Jesus addresses his mother as "Woman" from the cross, joining her to John in the new relationship shared by all disciples. Brown whispers like an observer at the edge of the crowd, listen and hear how Jesus is reinterpreting the way we relate to him, preparing us for that coming moment of revelation from the cross when he gives his mother to John and the beloved disciple to his mother. And he describes them, as we hear, not in terms of titles but in terms of relationships to him, his *mother, the disciple whom* he *loves, his kingdom is not of royal rankings but of recognizable human love.*

 NOW

This modern Cana is in a great hotel in Chicago but the large and noisy crowd is, as at that long ago feast, dressed in their best and thirsty for good wine. The banquet audience chuckles as, from the dais, Chicago columnist Irv Kupcinet introduces Joseph Cardinal Bernardin: *Doesn't it make you wonder when you hear that his mother and father are named Mary and Joseph?* Joseph smiles gently as he rises into the bright spotlight, nods to accept the applause, for these people are as glad to have him among them as their counterparts were pleased to have the young rabbi, Jesus, with them at Cana. The mother of each is present at a moment that underscores how each son cares for his mother but moves away from her, too, each seeking the path that allows them to do the work of the Father and each finding that it is a *Via Crucis*.

If the wine runs low at Cana, there is no chance that the supply will be compromised in Chicago. Both sons are aware of their mothers' presence and each acknowledges her and the advice she gives them about wine. These are not falsely emotional vignettes, not the catch-in-the-throat tremor of a hundred generations of clerics as they speak of their mothers; no, these are demonstrations, hard as the stones of the *Via Crucis*, of how each leaves home, shedding the dutiful son role cherished by their mothers, to take on backbreaking missions in the world at large. If Jesus slakes the thirst of the wedding guests at Cana,

Joseph makes the banquetgoers leave their wine unquaffed during the moments in which he stands before them. Maria is seated nearby, smiling and nodding, yes, in one moment her crimson-vested son is doing her proud in a vast and glittering ballroom and, in the next, she is not sure who he is or where she is. But she is mother enough, and mindful of the beverage, to advise her son, as he now tells the crowd, *Don't drink too much wine tonight, no good for you.* It is a wonder far smaller than that of Cana, yet it gladdens the hearts of the guests and makes the waiters smile as, under the spell of his softly spoken words, they stand, napkins over their arms, holding tight to the wine that the guests forget to request.

Joseph has redefined his relationship to his mother by deepening his relationship with the Father who is calling him toward a public dying with Chicago, as Midwest as Jerusalem is Mideast, as Calvary. He sees that his mother is cared for by the Little Sisters, he visits her every day, but it is the will of the Father that he seeks as he leaves her behind.

Maria is left as a widow in lean Depression times when Joseph's father, come to South Carolina with his brothers to work the stone quarries, dies when Joseph is six and his sister Elaine is four. They seek refuge from the ravages of the bad times as Jesus' family did the ravages of Herod. Their Egypt is public housing and Joseph and his seamstress mother meet their first fork in the road when Joseph decides against using the scholarship he wins for premed studies at the university in order to enter the seminary instead. *If you leave,* Maria asks, *will you be able to get it back?* Joseph, wearing a black suit made by his mother, takes that first decisive step away from her who surrenders him to it. This is the initial step on the road that leads away from Columbia, South Carolina, into the great world where he seeks what he prays for, to know and do the will of the Father.

And now that road has turned into the Way of the Cross and there are, as at Calvary, two parts to this cross, one to be fastened as a crosspiece to the other. The first of these is given to Joseph at the very beginning of the three-year ministry that, like the ministry of Jesus, leads to public death. Joseph is weighed down with the staggering crossbar of false accusation, later to be fastened to the upright stake of cancer. As he makes his way under this shameful burden, Joseph visits Maria every day, and what is it, we may ask, that they communicate through their eyes, how much does Joseph fill in with these glances or how much does she pick up with her own, of the suffering he is experiencing? Joseph meets his mother not once but many times along his *Via Crucis*, unwilling to tell her what he suspects that she, invested with the wisdom of all the black-shawled mothers watching at every crossroad of Italian history, knows already or senses in some way or other. *Do not trouble her*, the doctors say, *she does not understand, it would only confuse her*. And so Joseph, bearing now this bowsprit cross on his own back, searches the eyes of his mother, this witty and talented woman who knows him in one moment and does not in the next. *What is it you do?* she asks one afternoon. *Why, mother, I work for the Church*. She nods, *They don't pay very well, do they?* He smiles and tells the story many times, for Maria, communicating in a manner that in the same sweet instant seems unknowing and yet deeply knowing, what is she telling me beneath this loving concern, if not that she grasps that there is a price on his life, that the Father's will exacts a great cost from both mother and son?

The Fifth Station:
Simon Carries the Cross
for Jesus

Then

We pause to watch a scene as concrete as a news report in which eye-witnesses are interviewed about a transaction that is more physical than metaphysical. The differences are a function of where the observer is standing or because of word of mouth information, mis-shapen as it races along the sparking fuse of street gossip, but who, we wonder, touched the taper of first telling to it, is it this man or that woman, are they not at the very edge of the surging crowd no more than an arm's length away from Simon of Cyrene as the guards force him to carry the cross for the condemned Jesus? Who first grasps what is going on, catching the wide uncertain eyes of Simon as the soldiers single him out and press him into their service? But it is over as quickly as it is begun, and with as little notice as the substitution of a

player in a modern athletic contest, a small moon of an incident with no gravity to pull the tide of our attention away from the noisy and compelling central spectacle.

The commentators tell us little of the background of this helper who so mysteriously enters the great mystery afloat on the sighs and shouts of the crowd. Some say he is Jewish, for, then as now, Jews were sent to colonize in just such lands as this province Cyrene on the great reef of Africa. Others contend that his origin makes him an African, while still other scholars say that his name gives him away as Greek. Matthew, Mark, and Luke tell us that this man, yoked into immortality by the crossbar transferred to his shoulders, is Simon, but John does not mention him or the incident at all. Scholars have wondered for years about whether he existed or was invented, as one of their number, Reinach, suggests, to symbolize dramatically the words of Jesus (Mark 8:34; Luke 9:23): "If anyone wills to follow me, let him deny himself and take up his cross and follow me."

While Father Brown assures us that "Simon is undoubtedly an historical figure," and acknowledges that the words about following Jesus might naturally echo in the minds of the gospel writers, he adds that we know little about Simon beyond the fact that the people recognized him when he was stopped on his way into the city and made to carry the crossbar that had been fitted to Jesus' shoulders after his sentencing. Although it is clear from studies of crucifixion customs that he did not pick up the back of a fully fashioned cross, as this incident is rendered on a thousand canvases, no one knows where he is found in this procession, nearby or far behind Jesus, in this dramatic public revelation of the cost of discipleship (pp. 913–917).

Why, Brown asks, if the Greek words used by the writers are accepted, is Simon "coerced into his role of taking up or bringing the crossbeam?" Objections are made to Simon's carrying out this assignment because of the well-known Roman practice of forcing the con-

demned man to bear his cross unaided to the place of execution. *And would the Romans, who were known, according to the historian Josephus, for not forcing their conquered subjects to violate their own national laws, make a Jew carry out this grim work on Passover? Why, indeed, would these Romans, who mock and abuse Jesus, suddenly try to lessen his burden by shifting it to Simon? It is possible, Brown observes, that the Roman soldiers, aware that Jesus is weakened by their flogging him, "were afraid that he would die before he got to the place of execution and the sentence of the governor carried out." That this pragmatic reason governs their pressing the first broad-shouldered man to come into view to carry the cross because of the "dangerous weakness" of Jesus gains support from "the surprise shown over the swiftness of his death once he is crucified (Mark 15:44; John 19:33)."*

Simon descends from Calvary into history, leaving tracks filled in by the drift of time. Is he, as some suggest, a convert to Christ's way? Is he integrated artfully into a series of three, a device employed regularly in Gospel stories and used as an association to strengthen tradition's own memory? If so, Simon is grouped imaginatively with the good thief who merits sudden grace on his cross (Luke 23:40–43) and with the centurion who receives sudden light to proclaim the innocence of Jesus from below him (Luke 23:47). What we do know is that John does not mention him at all because he is less concerned with hard historical fact than he is with his grand theme of the theological significance of Jesus' authoring and controlling his own death.

Writing a generation and more later than the other evangelists, John gives a finely crafted drama in balanced acts of the unfolding meaning, from trial to death, of this journey to the cross. John rejects Simon's role in assisting Jesus in carrying the cross not to challenge the historical record but to sharpen the theological meaning of this crowning event in the life of the Messiah. Notions as wild as those on tabloid covers have, however, fluttered down through history to explain why Simon is missing from John's account. In one tale, Jesus exchanges places with Simon at this station and stands at the edge of Calvary laughing as this substitute is crucified in his place. Another contends that John is playing on his readers' possible recollection of the Old Testament Isaac who "carried the wood for his own sacrifice (Genesis 22:6)" so that Jesus stands in the tradition of the suffering servant of Yahweh (ibid).

A theological motive is "more probable," Brown tells us as, to the clink of armor, the groan of leather, and the off-key jangle of a sack of spikes dropping to the ground, the procession stops at this place of the skull, this true north of the Messiah's calling that is staked out by the upright column of the cross already driven into the earth. "John's Christology," Brown tells us, "has no room for Jesus' needing or accepting help. The basic principle of John 10:17–18 comes into play: 'I lay down my life . . . no one has taken it away from me; rather I lay it down of my own accord.' " *John also underscores the sovereignty of Jesus in the garden when the soldiers shouldering toward him to arrest him suddenly fall back to the ground (18:6). Jesus does the same in his challenge to the high priest about why he is being questioned (18:21) and in his telling Pilate* "You have no power over me at all (19:11)." *John invests the historical details with theological substance that removes any thought that Simon is necessary as an agent in Jesus' completing the work of his Father. That "John's omission of Simon," Brown concludes, "was to emphasize Jesus' control or authority in the crucifixion may be hinted at in Justin's statement (Apology 1:35.2) that when Jesus was crucified, he applied his shoulders to the cross, a statement that he accompanies with the citation from Isaiah 9:5(6):* 'On his shoulders rests the authority/rule (p. 917)."

John is also about his Father's business, for his main goal is not to tell a story but to orchestrate a theologically pure understanding of this great mystery in which Jesus freely and of himself authors this work that fulfills the will of his Father. Do not clutter your imagination with the other cast members, however colorful. These supporting actors, from the high priests to Pilate to the soldier who raises his hammer above the spike, deceive themselves, as we do ourselves, with any thought that they, rather than Jesus himself, deliver him to his destiny. At this station, a muddy finger reaches into the waters as the occasion for, but not the cause of, the slight shift in the course of the swiftly flowing river. The energy for that movement rises from the heart of the rushing waters, from the soul of the river as it seeks its own way to the sea.

 Now

Joseph stands at a point in his journey at which he understands that his calling is not of the world of ecclesiastical glory, nor of merely being acted upon by external forces or by internal illness but rather to be the author himself of the will and work of his Father. He does not lack for those who would help him, indeed, who do help him, who pride themselves on the opportunity and long to help him even more in the precious time they share. But each and every one one of us—because I count myself and my wife, Sally, among them—learn that we are bit players, that, save perhaps for Kenneth Velo and Scott Donahue, we can relieve Joseph of a fraction of his burden at best. No one can relieve Joseph of his cross because the crossbar is his own back, fragmenting as he bears it, driving electric spikes into its nerves whenever he reaches too far for something at his desk or makes a movement whose torque tears at the egg-carton bone. This crossbar cannot be handed off, this half-eaten casing collapsing on the nerves like a redwood on a power line, this pain so deep within his own being as to be one with his consciousness of himself and yet incommunicable to others. Joseph accepts this but senses how he stands alone on this side of the gulf of pain and that family and closest friends stand on the other. If he feels their love and their desire to help, he learns something else about the isolating impact of pain.

Does Joseph see in the eyes of his helpers what Jesus sees in the eyes of those in the crowd who weep for him as he passes? Does Joseph keep control of his suffering because the eyes of his helpers often reveal how upset they are by the sight of the very suffering they pray to lessen? Joseph is suffering intensely alone because his friends and helpers so desperately need him to be free of its grasp, to be among them as he always has been, Joseph holds their happy world together, and they wish to relieve his suffering but they need him still to deliver them from their own.

"They feel better," Joseph tells my wife one day in the December before he dies, angling himself cautiously into the silver Buick he drives by himself to the diocesan offices, "they feel better when I am there." Joseph understands what John emphasizes about Jesus, for he senses that in his years of praying to allow Jesus to take over his life, he has contracted freely for the loneliness that only the loving can know when those they love, mothers and brothers, are blurred faces at best in those that cluster around him, in those that draw closer to him the closer he draws to Calvary, the crowds of the needy and the suffering who bring their sick and their infants to him in every public place he enters, who wait for and surround him as he leaves his cathedral or any church.

Often they do not speak, these men and women wordlessly bringing him their casks of private woe, opening them as the wise men did their treasure chests, spreading this wealth of sorrow before him, for they offer the gift of the finely hammered sorrow of their years, *take this and, if you cannot make it into joy, make it less painful for us to bear.* They place their babes against his arms, they reach from behind to surprise him with their gentle touches, prayers really, *heal us and make our children safe*—and

Joseph stands serene in their midst, making little of himself, embarrassed that he is the center of so much attention, knowing that these good people perceive in a glass darkly what he sees more clearly with every step: that he carries his cross alone, that it is as inseparable from himself as his tortured back is, that he is doing the work, dazed by pain and puzzled by so much attention, that God gives him to do and that the place of the skull is not far off.

Nonetheless, he is the pastor, the shepherd of this flock and he must welcome them, must hide his pain even from the helpers like Kenneth Velo and Scott Donahue, and the nuns, like Sister Lucia, who care for him every day; he must remember their feelings as he realizes that, having begun this *Via Crucis* by himself, he must finish it by himself as well. He must exercise control as fully and as long as he can for the sake of his beloved family of helpers who inhabit the mystery but stand outside it at the same time, all of us, friends and helpers who witness but cannot share in the work Joseph does—and must do—for himself in letting Jesus take over and fill his life. Joseph writes of this during a retreat he makes with Bishop Robert Morneau of Green Bay, Wisconsin, his Simon helper for a few days of reflection and prayer partway through this three-year public life between the first false accusation and his final illness. He notes on the top sheet of a pad of lined paper, in his flowing, well-practiced penmanship, *Revelations 3:20—giving up,* and, below that, *Luke 1—annunciation—trust.* And then he opens his soul: *I want desperately to open the door to let the Lord in so he can take over my life completely. Yet I seem unable to do so. I let him come in partway; I talk with him but I am afraid to let him take over. Why?*

He meditates, turning over the soil that he has sifted many times before: *I want to succeed; I want to be acknowledged as one* who succeeds; I am very upset when I read or hear criticism about my decisions/actions. This drive causes me to want to control *things; make them come out "right."*

And now he has words for any who would help him: *For this reason, I tend not to put full confidence in people until they have proved their competence.*

Joseph wants to pare away the self that keeps him, as he sees it, from allowing the Lord to be his only Simon: *Conceptually, I know he can and should be trusted. It is his Church; nothing happens that is beyond his purview, etc. Yet I seem unwilling to let go. Is it because, at times, I fear that his will may be different from mine and that if his will wins out I will be criticized? Is it because, psychologically and emotionally, I have simply not been able to let go?*

If the evangelist John omits Simon to show that Jesus is in control of his life and his laying it down, Joseph measures his Simons carefully because he grasps, not without rue, that he must be in control of his own life and his living it out to the end. Joseph sees his capacity to keep control of his life not as an asset but as a hindrance to his allowing the Lord to enter his life as a Simon, indeed, *the* Simon that he can trust completely.

But he is aware of the needs and expectations of those who crowd around him. *Is part of the cause of this the fact that so many people each day make demands on me? Is it because their expectations are so numerous, direct, and personal that I cannot free myself from their pressure? Is there a certain pride that causes me not to risk letting go? Am I paralyzed to some extent by the fact that I am caught between the elements in the Church (who expect me to carry their banner) and the more conservative elements (including my peers and the Holy See) who expect me to support their agenda? Sometimes this tension causes me not to state what I* really *think.*

At this place along his way to Golgotha we ordinary people—innocent of the knowledge of good and evil whose details arch inch by inch across the desks of Church administrators as out of the glass bell of an old-fashioned stock ticker, and deaf to any calling to radical holiness—understand nonetheless the complexities of helping and being helped in life. These pale next to those of wanting to control ourselves or our lives or learning to dodge the grasp of those who offer us help not to free us but to gain some control over us. We shake off those who intrude on us in the guise of helping us, we move naturally toward the person—a parent, a teacher, a priest like Joseph— who gives without taking anything back or sending us an unexpected pay-on-demand bill. No wonder the crowds follow Joseph, no wonder they wish to touch him, making withdrawals rather than deposits without diminishing his goodness. The more Joseph seeks every day to let the Lord take over his life, the more light comes from him, like the yellow flicker of a porch lantern on a dark night, here, this is the way home, here is the place where you will be safe.

Jesus is the light and the truth, and Pilate, knowing better, chooses their opposites, washes his hands and walks into the ambiguous shadows of history. Perhaps we, who are Simons in one way or another to Joseph, identify better with the Cyrenean, this man suddenly bidden, as he returns to town after a day of work, to accept the role written for him long before in the Passion Play of salvation.

Chief among the Simons grouped at this station is surely Kenneth Velo, who is called from his daily diocesan administrative tasks by Joseph, as the fishermen were from their nets by Jesus, *Follow me more closely, share in my work and my destiny.* Kenneth accepts without hesitation and he is at Joseph's side when the false accusation explodes like a hand grenade and, three years later, he is with Joseph when the doctor hands down the death sentence and, as Joseph makes his way through the final months of his life, Kenneth is the caregiver who keeps watch with him until that bitter cold middle of the night when Joseph finally lowers his head and says, *It is finished.*

Sister Lucia is born in the same year as Joseph but half a world away in Poland. She is eleven when the Nazi blitzkrieg overwhelms that country and, in the victor's practiced way of sowing terror, breaks up her neighborhood and eventually sends her family on a Stations of the Cross that takes them in the worst of the war to Siberia and beyond. She moves on by way of Africa and India until she, who has had to mother the children younger than she, arrives in a convent run by the Felician Sisters in Mexico. Lucia professes her life to this order and is drawn into another journey that leads by stages to Chicago. That has been her destination all along and every harsh experience and small blessing has prepared her to do the work God has chosen for her, to manage the archepiscopal residence and to care for Joseph Cardinal Bernardin, to help carry the crosses of false accusation, fatal illness, and daily care and to be with him when he takes his last breath and the work of the Father is finished.

Let Father Velo and Sister Lucia stand for all those Simons who offer their help and support to Joseph, for Father Scott McDonald who is very close to Joseph and represents countless priests, and for Jim and Ellen O'Connor to stand, along with Phil Corboy and Mary Dempsey, and Kevin Dowdle near the top of an endless list of friends. There, too, are Father Al Spilly and Jeremy Langford, who help Joseph write his last book, *The Gift of Peace.* Let them stand for us all who, eager to help, learn what Simon does on the road to Calvary: that if Joseph does not shoulder his cross alone, it will not be carried at all. For the great mystery is embedded in the small mystery of this station, that Joseph, opening himself to Jesus, is given the same calling as

Jesus and, despite all who love and stand with him, he must fulfill that calling—enter that darkness and triumph over dread—without any of us, loved by all and yet conscious that this chalice of suffering could not be passed among his friends, that he must drink of it, including the dregs, by himself.

The Sixth Station:
Veronica Wipes the Face of Jesus

HEN

Few scenes are as familiar as this one in which a woman, given the name Veronica, approaches Jesus to touch a cloth of sympathy and relief to his blood- and sweat-streaked face. In the imaginations of artists, preachers, and generations beyond counting of believers, Jesus pauses and looks briefly into the eyes of this woman who, following her heart and forgetting herself, breaks gently through the shifting and wailing crowd, pushing aside the soldier's arm that is raised against her, creating, for a few fleeting seconds, an eye in the noisy hurricane to deliver a gift of human tenderness and to take back into the engulfing whirlwind the features of Jesus on the veil with which she has cleansed them.

So vivid is this scene that, even though it is not found in any of the Gospels, it has continued to reside in Catholic consciousness and to live on in the number of women who choose Veronica as the name by which they are known in religious life. Blink your eye and miss the shadow of someone vaguely like her that falls briefly across the background of Pilate's life and administration. In the ancient records termed the Acts of Pilate, *a woman named Berenice (Latin:* Veronica*) appears at the trial of Jesus before Pilate (#7) and identifies herself as the woman who touched Jesus' garment and was healed of a flow of blood (Luke 8:44). "Despite the meaning of her name,"* (bearer of the image), *"there is no reference to a portrait of Jesus," our guide tells us, noting that, according to M. R. James (*The Apocryphal New Testament, *(Oxford: Clarendon, 1953) "when Jesus met Veronica (but not on the way to Calvary) at her request, he imprinted the features of his face on a linen cloth (Brown, pp. 927, 928)."*

*Still, Veronica's deed has retained its pull across the centuries. Her proper place, we are told, is in the category of legend, (*Encyclopedia of Catholicism, *p. 1307), "an unverified popular story handed down from earlier times (*American Heritage Dictionary*)." This word flows out of the Latin* legenda, *meaning things to be read and, if it grants no stamp of verification, it does not totally rule out its possibility or, at the very least, of locating a foundational incident or group of incidents that justify symbolization in a story that, as in modern historical movies, is abridged or modified by dramatic license to convey its spiritual point. In this case, Father Brown, as limber and wise as G. K. Chesterton's priest-detective of the same name, notes that "although Luke does not contain the stories of Veronica and Jesus' three falls, his scene with the women contributes to the later devotion of the 'Stations of the Cross' (p. 927)."*

The spiritual meaning of the story of Veronica is found in its symbolism of and salute to the remarkable women who follow and accompany Jesus, especially in this climactic act of this Passion Play. These women move at his side on the way to Calvary, stand at or near the cross as Jesus is dying and just below it to receive and to prepare his body for burial. They are also there at first light when his tomb is found to be empty. Veronica leaves her image on the cloth of the Catholic imagination because her remembered action is a true symbol, a sacramental revelation, so to speak, of the bravery and tenderness of the women who play such an important role in the life of Jesus.

In addition to Mary who is the mother of Jesus, the legend accommodates several other women who are clearly named in the Gospel accounts. If Peter denies Jesus three times during the long night of his trials, there is no record of such a reaction on the part of any of these women. Let them step out of the shadows to tell us who they are as they reveal where they may be found in the larger narrative, of which the story of Veronica is an illustration.

It is not difficult, of course, to locate his mother Mary. But Mary Magdalene is also present, in overlapping Gospel accounts, throughout this Passion Play. She is there before and after the death of Jesus as well as at the burial and again when the tomb is found empty. In the Gospel narrative, we also meet Mary of Clopas, and Mary, the mother of James the Younger and Joses, along with Salome and Joanna, and, at these scenes that seem like family reunions, the "other women," those, described in the Gospels as following Jesus from Galilee, the same, Father Brown tells us, as the "many other women who had come up with him to Jerusalem (p. 1015ff.)."

At the roots of the legend of Veronica these same women keep vigil at the base of the cross not, as the Gospels make clear, as background figures nor as second-tier helpers who do the menial and secondary work in the community that clusters around Jesus. Even if we do not know every detail of their love and support for Jesus, there is no invisible shield keeping them at a distance. They are emotionally close to Jesus, they share intimate moments; they live, in a sense, his life with him, more like close family members who are free to laugh and *hug each other than choir members singing abstract Hosannas from across the sanctuary. They are not an audience any more than they are an entourage. They are friends together so that, even if we take the literal story of Veronica at historical discount, we are as comfortable in their human company as Jesus is. How typical, we might say, of masculine scholars who are so preoccupied with the failing Peter and the following John—and even the young man who loses his flapping garment as he flees from the garden of olives—that they take these women for granted, as if they should be there; isn't it their calling to be silent as they are of service? Perhaps we may take the name Veronica, from the Latin* verus *for* true *as a seal on the straightforward, unsentimental, and enduring love of the women we find everywhere in the life of Jesus.*

# Now

Joseph lives with women who cluster about him as naturally as they do around Jesus in the Gospel. They are not placed, as if by a modern public relations adviser, in roles designed for political advantage but are found at every point in Joseph's life and work. As we may imagine of the Marys and others in the Gospels, they understand and respond to him just as they are and just as he is, a virile, gentle man you might embrace or whose embrace you might receive without fear. These embraces are more than ceremonial among healthy people, they are the garden-variety blessings of investing in, rather than withdrawing from, the mystery of being human.

We remember the Veronica of legend for responding simply and humanly to Jesus, with the same unself-conscious spontaneity that characterizes the other strong women around Jesus. They do not ride the quick firework crescent of sensation but give quietly, drawing on the deep tranquil energy of their devotion to him. Let us not say less than that the women around Jesus love him, indeed, love him to the end, love him as women love even a man whom they can never marry, and if one is allotted only one great love in a lifetime, Jesus is that for them. Women also love Joseph and love him to the end, too, for they are present when Joseph is accused falsely and they are with him

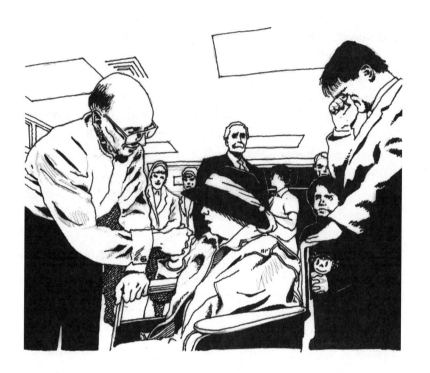

when he is sentenced to death, there as he bears his cross, and at his side at that cold dark midnight of his death.

Yes, and these women love him as women love a man and, for each, he is that one great love they will know, possess and yet never fully possess, and they love him with full hearts. His sister Elaine loves him purely and she is there at all the moments of triumph and trial in Joseph's life. She recalls how self-effacing he is even as the little boy who is her big brother, how bright and hardworking he is, how he strives to use his great gifts of intellect as fully as possible and of how he never complains.

One evening when he is not yet ten, Joseph falls and breaks his arm outside but conceals it because he does not want to add to the heavy burdens his mother already carries. He shields Elaine from any knowledge of it, covering and carrying it to the side, slipping into bed without telling anyone, even though the bone punctures the skin. But he cannot control the pain or the involuntary sobs he makes as he vainly tries to position himself in bed so as to bother no one. The women then in his life, his mother and sister, uncover his injury and see that it is treated and Elaine bears away an image of a devoted brother who puts love of others before his own pain or discomfort.

Joseph is that way on the last weekend of his life, when he is already at Calvary, exhausted, in need of someone to bathe his face and yet moved so by the visit of his sister's children that he does not want to disappoint them, does not want to miss these last moments with them and so tries to hide the fatigue that in the endgame of cancer no man can obscure. He cannot keep his head up, he drifts, grips the chair, *No, I'm fine,* as he tries, at their beseeching, to watch television with them. They bear away the image of an uncle giving what he can of his hospitality to them, only realizing later that they are making this station with him as they see in memory the image of his gaunt and pain-lined yet willing face.

And there are other women who stick with Joseph, finding their lives changed unexpectedly by their contact with him. They have never before met such a man; they bear this image of a man so at ease with himself, so transparent in his lack of defenses, so appealing in his manly way of living, that he is the love of their lives, too, leaving an image of a man who makes such gentle passage into their lives that they are astounded that he can give so much without taking anything away from them. No, he is not an ascetic who disowns the world and its women, no, he is very much in this world, in love with it just as it is, a profoundly human man who can give and accept love without ever compromising himself or others.

We have already met Sister Lucia, as self-effacing in caring for Joseph as she is competent in supervising his residence, bought by the poor Catholics of the nineteenth century so that their archbishop might live not so much in a way to befit himself as to befit them and the pride they take in living vicariously in a many-chimneyed redbrick home as grand as the governor's or that of any of the railroad barons and meat packers in the North Side neighborhood. Joseph transforms it from a worn and bare stage set into a warm and pleasant home for himself and the priests who work with him. Sister Lucia is there as Joseph has new paintings brought in from the archdiocesan major seminary, named *Mundelein* after a William Randolph Hearst–like predecessor who filled its buildings with European art and built himself a brick replica of Mount Vernon in which to take his ease when his duties palled. Sister Lucia remembers where and how the paintings are placed and hung, nods or not as Joseph looks toward her for an opinion. She attends to everything in the house in fulfilling this calling that she traveled out of war and around the world to discover.

And there is Ellen Gaynor, the nun-oncologist who sees him through the last year of his life, a professional who is taken by this patient, so unlike any other she has ever had, this gentle strong man who enters everybody's life without making claims or asking for privilege, this man who becomes so simply present, so fully and undefensively present that it is, as my wife, who knows him well for thirty years, puts it, like osmosis, he is suddenly there in an easy, calm manner that subtly but dramatically renews one's sense of the ordinary magic of friendship. He is not a man for a romance but he is not a man one ever gets over either.

And there is Claudia Dunne, the handsome raven-haired woman who weeps for all Chicago in the image picked up by the television cameras at Joseph's funeral. Claudia is the wife of George Dunne, former president of the Cook County Board and a prominent Democratic leader, and she comes often to pray in the Cardinal's private chapel and to take on any tasks that Joseph may assign, with a confident smile, to her.

There are also many others, some who care for his mother, others who help Lucia or perform other services—Ignacia, Josephine, Marina, Zita, and Mary Brian. The latter is the nun who is chief of his staff at the Superior Street diocesan headquarters. Each of them knows him in the same way and each of them knows him in a special way, this extraordinary man who so gently enters the lives of so many women who follow and care for him, as the women do for Jesus, right to the end.

The one longest with Joseph is Octavia Misoman, "Tanchie" as she is known, who accompanies him as his secretary out of his Galilee in Charleston to Atlanta, then to Washington, Cincinnati, and finally to his Jerusalem in Chicago. Ask Tanchie why she is always there, refusing other opportunities, always picking up and moving on, as we may suppose the women following Jesus do, out of one land and into another. Tanchie responds for all these loving women and for all those around Joseph, too, "Because I didn't want to be separated from all that goodness."

THE SEVENTH STATION:
Jesus Falls a Second Time

 Then

There is no record in the Gospels of these falls that are as familiar as the quick movement of Veronica who slips now back into the crowd, clutching the veil on which our collective memory of the brutality of the passion has encoded the bloody smears of Jesus' face. Are the unrecorded falls to be dismissed as a function of the confounded memories of early Christians or of the florid imagination of twenty centuries of artists? Or do these falls—for any man might go sprawling on the rough stones of this route away from the fortress of Antonia—provide a measure of something that, although recorded in the scriptures, often goes unnoticed?

There are events whose shape we readily make out from the way people react to them. A sharp intake of breath measures the depth and width—the surprise and impact—of a moment as sudden and defining as the deliberate crash of a 767 jet plane into Manhattan's World Trade Center. The look in a person's eyes reflects what we cannot see, the tide of assured love that washes through them. The hush that falls on a noisy crowd is just the right size to hold the horror of the racing car careening out of control and cartwheeling into the track wall. In the Gospels, we find evidence of reactions whose shape bears the outlines of these otherwise undocumented incidents, reducing their improbability, diminishing our willingness to believe that conflicting memories make the incident so vague as to be unknowable.

The reaction that often goes unacknowledged is that of the crowd as it shapes and reshapes itself around and beyond Jesus, its expansions and contractions revealing the stops and hesitations as he makes his way toward Calvary. The crowds are often described as a roiling mass of people, as unfeeling as an Old South lynch mob for the condemned man, setting a torrent of insults and ridicule washing over Jesus so that the weeping women of Jerusalem, whom he meets at the next station, seem, as do his own mother and a small handful of others, to be pure white chips borne on the boiling white water of the cataract.

But the crowd is not totally without feeling and the sympathy and sadness that Father Brown observes are large enough in themselves to accommodate the falls of Jesus and a young woman spontaneously reaching out to cleanse his face. "What impression," Father Brown asks, "do we get when we read in (Luke) 23:27: 'Now there was following him a large multitude of the people'? Although 'following him' is not necessarily a posture of discipleship, there is no prima facie suggestion of hostility . . . Indeed, Luke seems to assign a progressively favorable role to this portion of the Jerusalem population. If in 23:27 the 'large multitude of the people' is not itself said to mourn, it is associated with women who do mourn and are clearly sympathetic to Jesus (pp. 918–919)."

Father Brown goes on to note that as Jesus hangs on the cross (23: 35) . . . "'the people were standing there observing.' Although that description is noncommittal, the people are thus kept distinct from the three types of mockers whose description follows immediately (loc.cit.)." Brown notes of the scene after Jesus dies Luke's (23:48) report that "all the crowds that were gathered together for the observation of this . . . returned striking their breasts."

Brown also cites the apocryphal Acts of Pilate again. In 4:5 we read, "Now as the governor looked around on the multitudes of the Jews standing around, he saw many of the Jews weeping, and said, 'Not all of the multitude wish that he should be put to death.'" This picture, Brown observes, "would not strike ancient readers as implausible."

A statement as restrained as this by a scholar as astute as Father Brown changes our way of looking at this event. The compassion that Jesus feels gazing at the famished crowd is balanced by the compassion that this crowd feels looking at the condemned Jesus. Hearts are moved by the sight of this young rabbi, already worn down by beating and mockery, as he struggles past them. Can we rule out that sharp intake of breath and that sudden hush that not only measure the sympathy but the sight that inspires it in these people as they accompany Jesus along the Via Crucis? The sympathy for Jesus is documented by Luke and these people do not follow along because they want blood but because they are touched by the blood Jesus has shed and is yet to shed on the cross.

These people cannot be summoned from central casting as a bloodthirsty mob, as they are in so many representations of Jesus' passage to the place where he will die. These Jews are stirred by what they see him endure and that Jesus stumbles and rises again seems less invention than a rendering in miniature of the halting progress, marked perhaps by gashes and trauma that even tradition finds too painful to remember.

 # Now

Joseph falls the second time with no crowd around him. We understand this as a fall because he has barely regained his balance from that first fall under the impact of the false accusation that he sexually molested a seminarian under his care when he was archbishop of Cincinnati. The effects of that false charge linger deep in his body but he does not feel them when he is toppled the second time as his doctor, Warren Furey, insists that, even though Joseph feels well, he must endure a series of tests because of the symptoms of discolored urine that he reports to him.

Joseph feels that, by June 1995, he has put that incident behind him. While he is grateful when Steven Cook recants his accusation in March 1994, he feels that he has unfinished business with this young man who is never far from his thoughts. He wants, outside the gaze of the world, to reconcile with Steven, living now in Philadelphia, weakened by AIDS and cared for by a companion. Joseph at last makes the arrangements and on the last day of that year, he flies with Father Scott Donahue to Philadelphia where the meeting is arranged on the grounds of the major seminary outside the city at Overbrook. Steven is hesitant at first, still angry at the Church and at all religion, telling Joseph that, in his years as a male prostitute, he often threw the Gideon Bible found in every hotel room at the wall in disgust.

But there is something in Joseph's manner, in his earnest desire to reconcile that is measured finally in Steven's emotional acceptance of Joseph's invitation to celebrate the Eucharist together in the seminary chapel. First, Joseph anoints Steven and his companion with the Sacrament of the Sick and then he and Father Donahue concelebrate and the reconciliation is complete. Joseph, as I tell him, is a good shepherd. *What do you mean?* he asks. You go after the sheep that is lost in the brambles and leave the other ninety-nine of us on our own back here in Chicago. He chuckles, *I'm just doing what any priest should do.*

And now it is six months later and he is sitting in his doctor's office with Kenneth Velo and, against the tide that, since the reconciliation, carries him along buoyantly, Joseph feels the full force of its turn. *You have pancreatic cancer,* Furey explains calmly. *This illness is the event that will end your life.* Joseph remains calm, he understands what the doctor is saying, surgery, *Yes, yes, of course, yes,* and new treatments may give you more time. *How much time,* he asks his cancer specialist, Dr. Ellen Gaynor. *A year, perhaps more.*

It is all so fragile, he tells me and my wife a few days later, huddled close together in chairs in one of the parlors of his residence. He is changed from the man I had a drink with a week before, when my wife told him to be sure to keep his appointment with his doctor. He is gaunt and drawn and he is struggling to rise and right himself from the body blow of this diagnosis. He is just beginning the third year of the public ministry he entered into when he was accused, as unexpectedly as he has been diagnosed, and now he is standing free, sensing that his calling is becoming that which he has prayed for, that his life is following the pattern of that of Jesus, that what he writes in his retreat notes frames not only his earnest self-examination but the Eucharistic mystery of his remaining days.

What are the lessons in this for me *(and for our presbyterate)?*
I must always keep my eyes focused on Jesus. *He must be the* center *of my life. I must "let go" so he can work* in *me and* through *me. I must* visualize *the Jesus with whom I am intimately united, with whom I am in love (I must not be afraid to say this) as a* real friend, *a manly person who—even though he is God's son, shares the human feelings I experience: joy, sorrow, doubt, anxiety, etc.; one who* will *give me strength and support; one who understands and loves me despite my sins and weaknesses; one who will embrace me and give me comfort and a sense of security* if I let him. *In short, I must TRUST him completely. If I do I have nothing to fear—regardless of the pain and frustration of the present moment.*

The EIGHTH STATION:
Jesus Meets the Women
of Jerusalem

 Then

*Perhaps at no other point in this passage across the city do the streams
of so many sources intermingle, nourishing each other as they meld
together into a torrent that crumbles the banks of the land as it cuts a
new path through it. The mist that rises like winter breath from its
surface is that of the profound religious mystery in which every
human life, before and after this event, is set. Jesus pauses to speak to
a group of women from, as we have seen, the crowd that is not totally
unsympathetic to him. These are women we have already met as they
strike their breasts in a lament and mourning for Jesus that Father
Brown identifies as a tributary from Zecharia. They shall look on
him whom they have pierced and they shall beat themselves in*

mourning for him as for an only son, and grieve with grief as for a firstborn son (Zechariah 12: 10).

Before Jesus addresses them, we may examine with a wider lens the themes that concern the physician Luke as he assembles the sayings and puts down his narrative of the Passion. We have already felt the wave of sympathy that rolls across the multitude following Jesus as Luke artfully places before us figures who recognize Jesus' goodness and experience sadness at his suffering and approaching death. It is impossible to grasp the underlying sympathy, rather than anger, in Jesus' words to these women if we do not appreciate the context into which Luke invests his meaning.

We have already seen the stranger Simon of Cyrene shoulder the crosspiece. He is only one of a grouping of three, a scriptural device used often by Luke to establish his dominant theme. He allows us to see the women weeping and lamenting for Jesus and shortly introduces the wrongdoers who are crucified on either side of Jesus. One of them, known to us as the good thief, is promised paradise this day. Beneath the cross Luke places another figure, the centurion whose heart is so moved that he proclaims that Jesus is indeed a just man. This trinity of responses establishes and accomplishes Luke's purpose. As our guide reminds us before we turn back to Jesus as he speaks to these women, "If for Mark the passion manifests human failure and evil . . . for Luke God's love, forgiveness, and healing are already present throughout the passion . . . Simon emerges in Luke in the stance of a disciple; not all the people are hostile to Jesus since a multitude follows him and the Jerusalem women lament for him; one of the two wrongdoers . . . will be made victorious with him; a Roman centurion will become a spokesman of Jesus' innocence; the crowds will be so touched . . . that they will beat their breasts in penance; and the women from Galilee . . . will see his death from afar but later see the tomb emptied by his victory (p. 931)."

Yet the words of Jesus to these women—even though retranslated and explained and laid on a lecture table before us like dried-out scrolls whose low and grating whisper of a time no harsher than our own, and of men and women we might find in our family albums— still cause us to pull back at this negative prophecy about to be fulfilled in Jerusalem.

We can easily see the parallel between Jesus' passage out of Jerusalem and his entrance a few short days before. A multitude of the people are with him in his moment of triumph and in these hours of loss. They include women just such as these and, against the waving palms and shouts of welcome, Jesus addresses these women personally and collectively as Daughter Zion, and now, in Luke, Daughters of Jerusalem. The writer is following a stream that trickles out of the headwaters deep in the Old Testament, in which women are addressed, as Father Brown explains, "as representatives of the nation or the city in oracles of joy or woe (p. 921)." There we find Daughters of Israel (2 Samuel 1:24) as well as Daughter Zion (Zephaniah 3:14; Zechariah 9:9) and Daughters of Jerusalem (Song (Canticle) 2:7). This way of speaking is not negative, we learn, but rather identifies their fate with that of the great city itself.

Jesus has previously spoken the words Do not weep *to the widow of Naim as she grieves for her daughter (Luke 7:13) and, later, to those lamenting the loss of the daughter of the ruler (Luke 8:12). The context is imminent death, as it is now, but, if in these words Jesus is about to turn their mourning into joy by bringing renewed life to the dead, he does something very different here as he directs their grief away from his own death, "toward the death of the city and its inhabitants (loc. cit.)."* Do not weep for me . . . for yourselves weep. . . . *This washes down on us from falls far up in the biblical mountain, from Jeremiah where the Lord calls the women to mourn over Jerusalem, a dirge is heard from Zion, "How ruined are we and greatly ashamed . . . Hear, you women . . . teach your daughters this* dirge and each other this lament" (9:16–18). Jesus speaks through these women to the city that rejects him.

Father Brown helps us to understand these words, so imbued with out canceled out sympathy of Old Testament prophecy that they still put our teeth on edge, as the evangelist Luke's mode of saying that "those responsible for the execution of God's son will be punished, even in the next generation, through the destruction of Jerusalem (p. 931)." These are powerful prophecies—that it is better not to be born, and better not to bear life, under the shadow of God's just punishment for what Jerusalem does to his prophets and to him. They find their antecedent in those spoken hardly an hour earlier by the crowd to Pilate: His blood be upon us and our children and We have no king but Caesar. Yet, there is a crucial difference, as Father Brown observes, "those self-convicting statements placed respectively on the lips of all the people and of the chief priests are much harsher in their context and import than the reluctant oracle reported from Jesus' lips by Luke (p. 931)." That these rueful words are spoken to women who lament denies that the coming devastation will be deserved by all on whom it will fall as randomly as the rain. Luke wants us to understand that "not all were hostile and leaves open the possibility that the God who touched the hearts of Simon and one of the wrongdoers, and of the centurion may in turn have been touched by the tears of those who lamented what was being done to Jesus (pp. 931–932)."

 # Now

Joseph is in the midst of the multitude during the three-year
public ministry he is allotted, almost to the day, after the false
accusation of sex abuse strikes him like an assassin's bullet in
November 1993. That bullet, bearing the markings of those who
are uncomfortable with Joseph for who he is and what he
preaches in the public forum, leaves its poisonous residue even
after it is removed. Joseph bears within himself a wound that no
recantation of the charges can heal. Is this the spoor set loose
within his inner being, his guts, as we say of a good man's bravery, that come finally to deadly term within him? It hides within
him in these three years just as so many of his fellow high priests
who criticize him hide behind the buttered phrases and the
affected kinship of clerical culture that they extend to him during this time.

Among these high priests, as we shall see, are brother cardinals who conspire against him beneath their white hair and
behind their sea-blue eyes and their hearty, *How are you, Joe, and
how is your mother?* But, if some of his brother bishops and cardinals are seeking and, indeed, finding ecclesiastical power,
Joseph speaks as one having authority. The crowds follow him,
even hostile high priests recognize that, among the bishops at
large, he and not they, for all their power games, is the one who
is trusted, the one appraised as credible and fair and a keeper of

his word. If their applause at bishops' meetings is given with a sense of relief that he is able to lead them to agreements on important matters—to "save them" as one of them expresses it to me—the acclaim of the multitudes is spontaneous and heartfelt.

Joseph finds this so immediately after the false accusation makes worldwide headlines. He keeps to his schedule after the news conference at which the truth makes him free, but, recalling the condemning letter from a man he has counted as a friend, he, who wants to do the right thing in every way, cannot help but wonder how his brother bishops will react when he comes among them a few days later. Yet the multitudes acclaim him all along the way with a truck driver symbolizing the universal goodwill by leaning out of his cab and giving Joseph a big smile and a thumbs-up signal.

Joseph understands that he must take his destiny into his own hands, rejecting, as he does the first morning, the advice of all those who urge him to avoid speaking out, to defer to lawyers and to those who are skilled at covering broken china with public relations gloss. So he walks freely, meets with the press again at the bishops' meeting, finding that the truth that makes him free also keeps him free. And now he rises to speak to all the bishops and, if there is ambivalence in the hearts of some, there is unanimity in the Palm Sunday equivalent of the standing ovation with which they greet him. He is heartened when he returns to Chicago and, in the first church he enters for confirmation ceremonies, he is greeted in the same way. He is greatly comforted when, presiding at an African-American parish, he is not only warmly received but experiences, as the congregation sings traditional hymns about how this trouble will pass, the healing power of music ground so purely and sweetly out of a mill of unspeakable pain.

He walks through the Chicago streets in the evening for

exercise and, even dressed informally, is recognized and stopped by people of all faiths who are attracted to him because he speaks the truth. He will chat during these three years with groups of women beyond counting, some in great convention halls, others on street corners, and, finally, in hospital wards and waiting rooms. He is surrounded by the multitude wherever he goes. There are Veronicas among them who wish to take his likeness away in their cameras or in their imaginations. Others are petitioners who, as we have seen, want only to touch the hem of his garment or to ask for prayers for the sick or a blessing for a child.

Just how much the multitude loves Joseph is not clear until that warm June afternoon when the news flashes through the city that the Cardinal is ill, that his doctors, at his orders, will hold a press conference and explain his cancer, the Whipple procedure surgery that will be used, the follow-up treatment plan and the prognosis; one in five live for five years.

The noisy city holds its breath and stops for a moment. We can see now that its citizens are observing this station of the cross, pausing at this place where Joseph looks into the eyes of many and conveys the same message that is found deep inside Luke's account of this encounter with the women of Jerusalem. God's mercy is at work now in your lives, he loves you and will take you in his arms as Jesus longs to take Jerusalem in his to give it comfort and forgiveness. Joseph does not prophesy suffering to all those who gather around him at this station. He rather absorbs their pain and their longing, takes it into and unto himself, feels, as he tells me, that being a pastor in this way is the really important work for him and for all priests.

But this interlude is also filled with dread. One feels it across Chicago, this city that boasts of its sins and hides its heart but cannot do so now. For everyone is a centurion this day, attesting that Joseph is a true man, a just man, a holy man. And, everybody, wishing him well as he wishes them God's blessings and mercy, follows him uneasily in their hearts to the hospital on that Sunday afternoon. He visits his mother; does she sense that he must again be about his Father's business? He feels the sentence hanging over him, as the whole city does, that this is one stop in a journey he has not expected but that he embraces, this clearing where we all stand, our ambivalence hushed, as we somehow sense that we have no choice, that we must surrender this good and beloved man to the mystery, hid from our eyes and his, of his calling.

T͟H͟E NINTH STATION:
JESUS FALLS A THIRD TIME

 THEN

This third fall, so easy now to imagine, also goes unrecorded in the Gospels and, although it is in the tradition of the remembered places in the spiritual exercise of the Stations of he Cross, these latter have passed through many modifications and, although a powerful source of spiritual realization, they are not an exact account of what occurs as Jesus makes his way from the fortress, at which Pilate gives him over to the crowd, to the place of Golgotha where Roman soldiers give him to the cross. We sense, from the sympathy that Luke identifies in the crowd, the reactions of its members—Jewish save for the Roman guards—to the sufferings of Jesus. We cannot contend that, in the fashion of some mythical god, Jesus remains upright and indifferent to the scourging or to his stumbling on the worn stone path across the

city. If some spiritual writers meditate on a triumphant Jesus hurrying to fulfill the work and will of his Father on the cross, may the truth of this scene not be closer to the gritty face and profoundly human reactions we now witness, than to a Jesus immune to his own suffering and ours imagined in artworks in which a glorious Jesus attired in royal robes reigns from a cross made into a throne?

Great moments are often hidden inside events that seem routine or mundane. Is that all there is to it, we wonder of gatherings long imagined as unmistakable in their impact that, on closer examination, turn out to bear the dulled sheen of the everyday? A sad-looking man signs a piece of paper by candlelight in a quiet office and the Emancipation Proclamation puts an end to the long passion of American slavery. The event is understated but, if it cannot be underestimated, neither can the way it drained the deepest wells of anguish or took down generations from their crosses be portrayed adequately. That Jesus falls a third time is but an effort to symbolize the weight that he bore, the weight not so much of our sins as of all the suffering of all people before and after this day.

What is important in the scripture, as in a symphony, is the signature on this movement, this Pathétique of suffering humankind, this haunting and pervasive sense of a great sadness that spreads across the crowd and touches the heart of the centurion, this mood of sorrow and yet fulfillment that is symbolized in a stumble and fall and a getting up again. It is all real enough, as real as the suffering that, wise to the ways of time, flows through it and touches us all.

Still, if we cannot know everything, we know some things about the passion of Jesus that allow us better to stand in this multitude and to observe the details before they are so refashioned and elaborated on by others that it is almost impossible for us to find our way back to the true event. Let us look more closely at the crown of thorns that is placed on the head of Jesus in mockery of him as a king.

Since in describing the crown, the evangelists, Father Brown tells us, "mention thorns . . . in Christian thought it became an image of pain and suffering." In the Gospels, however, "there is no sense of torture; and the crown is part of the royal mockery, like the robe and the scepter (pp. 866–868)." In a piece of exegetical history that permits us to wipe away the airbrushing that has covered over the simple sad directness of this scene, we learn that scholars became curious about the nature of the crown and of this thorn plant mentioned in Matthew and John. Father Brown informs us that historians warn that the crowns of that period "were diadems or wreaths, not the crowns of later royalty (p. 866)." Scholars decided on the nature of the crown on the basis of their own investment in this crowning as an exercise in mockery or in torture.

The plant identified by the celebrated botanist, Linnaeus, and given a name associating it with the crown of Jesus—a plant of long thorns and green leaves—cannot, however, grow in the mountainous country around Jerusalem. Speculation and hypothesis have abounded, ranging from caps of thorns that mimic royalty to those that imitate the laurel wreathes of victors and rulers. Some scholars, Father Brown instructs us, contend that early readers of the Gospel would not have thought of thorns but rather of the acanthus plant, a thorny variety whose leaves, Father Brown suggests, the Roman soldiers could have plucked to weave a mock crown wreath. If we emphasize the pain of the crown, as in many depictions, including Martin Scorsese's carefully researched The Last Temptation of Christ (1988), we miss the "obvious Gospel theme of burlesquing royalty (loc. cit.)."

Yet this mockery turns soon enough to physical abuse, to the spitting and slapping and taunting of Jesus, revealing the hostility of the people aimed not at his claiming to be a king but that he presents himself as the son of God. Indeed, in the way this scene has been elaborated by commentators, Father Brown detects emphases this way and that by those who are using the material to accent some theological motif of their own. Here, in particular, he finds that early Christian reflection on the mockery of Jesus as the son of God, heaping blame on the Jews, developed, "sometimes with a polemic thrust (p. 869)."

 # NOW

Joseph's third fall is at home, on his own staircase, in the evening when the old house, with its thick walls and heavy doors, swallows every sound and his every call for help. He bears the cross in his back that, by Eastertime of this final year of his public ministry in 1996, causes him excruciating pain. He calls me early in April to report without complaint, *They tell me my back is much worse than I thought it was. I have a very severe case of osteoporosis and I had another compression fracture last week. They are concerned about the curvature, they say it is 36 percent now.*

He can barely balance the cross as we discover, as we look into each other's eyes when I visit, that, although we have always been the same height, he is now six inches shorter than I am, bowed by this cross whose weight I can feel even if I can see it only in its effects. Joseph is cheerful. I have written the text for a book of photographs taken of him by John White of the *Chicago Sun-Times* and he is quietly pleased with the results. It seems a pitifully small gift to offer him but he smiles and speaks of Dr. Leonard Cerullo, the renowned neurosurgeon who has been cautioning him about any efforts to remedy his back with surgery. But Joseph maintains control of his life and seeks other opinions. He smiles, *Yesterday and today I feel better.* Then he sighs, measuring the painful steps he must yet make, *Somehow, some way, this will be resolved.*

But it is that evening when the full weight of his cross unbalances him as he climbs the carpeted stairs in his own residence and sends him sprawling. His cane tumbles down the steps below him. Sister Lucia has finished cleaning up the kitchen, turned off its light, and walked to the convent residence across the back garden. Bishop Raymond Goedert, his vicar-general, amiable, hardy, and hardworking, is behind the heavy door of his room, as is Kenneth Velo, just a few steps up and a few feet down the second-floor corridor. Nobody can hear Joseph as he calls for help, the full measure of his illness and the full weight of the cross of his damaged back fall upon him and, pausing to ease the pain and to catch his breath, he steels himself and begins, an inch or perhaps two at a time, to pull himself up the stairs.

It is slow progress and the starburst shells of pain dizzy him and blot out everything but his powerful concentration on the next movement. Joseph reaches the landing, can find no grip that does not ignite the pain in his back, hears a clock chime, its sound as muffled by the old house as his own voice as he inches along towards his own room. He drags himself across the sill, reaches up, gropes in the dark for the phone on his desk, knocks it to the floor, manages to call Kenneth Velo, his closest aide, his friend, the first and finest of the sons he has made of the priests who work and live with him. He slumps, rolls over, is lying helpless on his back as Kenneth Velo and Bishop Goedert rush to bear him in their arms to his bedroom and to call for help.

T̶ʜᴇ TENTH STATION:
Jesus Is Stripped of His Garments

 Then

As much is presumed as may be presented visually in the paintings and carvings of the Stations of the Cross for, as we arrive at Golgotha, we can see this place—its rock crown so like a skull jutting half out of its burial place, and there, driven into this bone is the stake of the waiting upright part of the cross, and near it the soldier executioners hefting the tools they need for this grimmest of tasks, and, not far from them, the crowds converging on this slope just as morning yields to afternoon. We have seen a hundred versions of this, some lurid in detail, some carved down to spare symbols. What do we know of this place where we have visited so many times before?

This gnarled and rocky knob is called—both in Semitic (Golgotha) and in Greek (kranion), meaning skull or cranium—the place, as it is often rendered, of the skull. Father Brown puts aside fine points to seek out the meaning of harsh but familiar promontory. All the forms, he tells us, are "reconcilable with the suggestion that the appearance of the site was similar to a skull because it was a rounded knoll, rising from the surrounding surface (p. 957)." Because John tells us that a tomb was to be found there (19:41) "many have thought that the entrances to cavelike tombs may have supplied the knoll with facelike aspects (loc. cit.)." It is grim and stark by any account and if, as it has been supposed, it is elevated, it serves the Roman purpose of using crucifixions as public warnings. What is now left of this elevation, in Brown's best judgment, is contained within the Church of the Holy Sepulcher.

The tortured journey is now over and the guards prepare to be executioners. Scholars ask, in the light of Gospel descriptions, whether, after Jesus is mocked, crowned, and clothed in what passes for a royal robe but may be nothing more than the borrowed cloak of a guard, he is relieved of these clothes and dressed again in a simple tunic. "Normally," Father Brown tells us, "the criminal, carrying the lateral beam of the cross behind his neck with his arms fastened to it, would go naked to the place of crucifixion, being scourged as he went. . . . In having the final disrobing of Jesus only at the place of execution (Mark 15:24), the evangelist may reflect a local concession that the Romans made to public nudity (p. 870)."

Jesus' tunic, known to us as a seamless garment, is removed in the kind of preparatory ritual of which faint but distinct traces may be found in modern executions, and he is offered wine to drink before he is placed on the cross. "The Roman soldiers," Father Brown explains, "give him oinos (sweet wine) mixed with myrrh and gall, but he does not take/drink it. . . . At the end, after Jesus' cry of desolation, 'someone' among the bystanders fills a sponge with oxos (coarse, bitter wine, vinegary in taste), fits it on a reed, and gives it to him to drink (Mark 15:36; Matthew 27:48). This is done in a context of mockery, *but it is not clear that the action itself is a mockery. We are not told whether Jesus drank it (loc. cit.)."*

Jesus' refusal to drink of the first offering, according to our guide, underscores Jesus' commitment to giving himself totally, drinking the cup given to him by his Father to the dregs. We also hear echoes of the psalms, especially 69:22: And they gave for my bread gall and for my thirst they gave me to drink vinegar. But these shimmer away in the intensity of this moment when the final action of the drama is about to begin and Jesus, stripped of his garments, stands waiting for the executioners to do their work and to complete his.

# Now

Joseph is stripped of his garments in time and yet wears a seamless garment into eternity. He is stripped of his privacy, stripped to the bone of his inner self by the widely broadcast charge that he had sexually abused seminarian Steven Cook at his residence in Cincinnati. Joseph is mocked and ridiculed by those critics who have worked for so many years and in so many ways to spread rumors that he leads a double life and indulges in perverse sexual behavior. Such wild accusations continue long after his death and, like radioactive waste, spit out their old poisons in the new century. Those who take on the mocking roles in this Passion Play establish Web sites on which they recycle their familiar accusations that grow out of the fantasies of men who gratify their own perverse needs by downing and demeaning another man.

Joseph is stripped of his garments by the eager coverage of CNN of charges they accept without investigation and of evidence they accept without examination.

He is stripped of his garments by the silent invasion of cancer whose seeds, in the judgment of many who know him, are set loose by the death-ray sex abuse accusation aimed directly at him. No person is more modest or self-effacing than Joseph, no person more concerned with being proper while remaining engagingly human. Yet a sudden ravaging illness assaults every citadel in a modest man's life and he must surrender to the instruments of those who, even in having him submit to their scalpels and probes, cannot strip away the dignity of bearing that, unclothed to the universe of medical examination, he projects effortlessly from within.

He meditates on the words with which St. Paul refers to Jesus: *He did not think his kingship something to be clung to but emptied himself*. . . . And so Joseph, praying to be united with Jesus, sees his calling as one in which, out of love for the Lord and service to the Church, he must embrace this Mystery of loss in which he empties himself, letting go of all that he possesses, of all that he would cling to about being a Cardinal-Archbishop, the better to bear this illness and death that await him in the darkness just beyond these last days. He lets go of all that he has planned to do, all but a few last projects that he may yet complete before he finishes his Father's work and his own.

But he is also stripped of his garments by men in whom he has had confidence, men with whom he has worked for years in the Church, some of the high priests who, even before his illness, seek to blunt his influence in Rome in order to increase their own. Joseph is peacefully and patiently aware of this, telling me one day that Cardinal Law is the most influential man in the American Church, that Bernie, as he calls him, is calling the plays in the American Church. *I am at peace,* he says, *because I intend to continue to do my work in the way I always have and I truly believe that will stand up in the long run.*

Still, when he becomes ill, he senses how quickly some of these high priests move to make sure that he cannot have any influence over his successor in Chicago and that his voice and views on the American Church will not be heard in Rome. Bernard Cardinal Law of Boston has ingratiated himself with the Pope by cooperating in John Paul II's efforts to restore the authoritarian hierarchical Church that was returned to its original collegial form at Vatican Council II. Joseph learns that Law is making every effort to have Francis George, a gracious and dutiful man now bishop in Yakima, Washington, made an archbishop in Portland, Oregon, so that he will have that rank when Joseph dies, making it easier for Cardinal Law to have him named as Bernardin's successor as archbishop of Chicago.

Joseph is stripped of his garments when the same high priest decides, in conversations with other United States cardinals, to cut Joseph out of the conference calls that they regularly share to discuss matters in the American Church. Yet Joseph, praying that he may empty himself, launches one last project, *Common Ground*, through which he hopes that Catholics who have differing views on the meaning of Vatican II's reforms may enter into a dialogue so that they can resolve their differences and stand together in the Church.

Joseph is stripped again of his garments by Cardinal Law and James Cardinal Hickey of Washington, D.C., who, breaking the age-old protocol that cardinals never criticize each other in public, immediately issue statements taking Bernardin to task, suggesting that *Common Cause* is superfluous, that all that counts is adherence to the orthodox teachings of the Church. He admits the hurt of this to me in his rooms one night a few weeks before his death. *You know that, if a new Pope came in who looked at things a little differently, they would change their minds overnight.*

And Joseph is stripped of his garments when, his cancer having returned, he mounts one last flight to Rome to recommend a progressive bishop to become his co-adjutor and to succeed him on his death. In Rome, he is treated with cordiality but with stares that tell him that he can no longer wield any influence, that he is indeed stripped of everything by officials who think it odd that any cardinal would be willing to share or surrender even a small portion of his authority while he is still alive. *I would never do it*, a Vatican official tells him, *I would never do it, why do you think such things?*

He is stripped by that trip and by the increasing gulf that opens between himself and other powerful prelates that leaves him out of the loop of influence in the power structure of American Catholicism. Yet, early in September, the President of the United States awards him the Medal of Freedom and, on the same afternoon, his voice breaking because of the strain of his illness, Joseph delivers one last lecture at Georgetown University on the Church's right to participate in the debate on public policy. He returns to Chicago, fully aware that his hour has come, that he must use his energy to write a short final book, *The Gift of Peace*, and drink then the cup that the Father has given him to complete his work and his life.

The Eleventh Station:
Jesus Is Nailed to the Cross

 Then

Accounts of the crucifixion of Jesus are found in all the Gospels (Mark 15:24; Matthew 27:35; Luke 23:33; John 19:18) and yet there is much about the death of Jesus that we do not know. Archeological investigations and ancient documents depict a variety of crucifixion styles, describing how this brutal form of execution is employed to humiliate and shame the condemned person, lining the crosses along the great travel roads, You who pass by, look at these dead and know the swift justice the state metes out to wrongdoers. *The executed are often hung at eye level, where the birds dart at the dead and dying while animals gnaw at their feet and passersby speak to or berate them before looking away. It is thought that the Medes and Persians first employ this means of slow, painful, and public death on*

a mass scale and bequeath this bloody punishment to the Greeks. Under Alexander the Great it becomes a common practice.

Father Brown suggests that the "Carthaginian relatives of the Phoenicians practiced crucifixion, and contact with them in the Punic Wars seems to explain its spread to the Romans. Crucifixion of Jews became their policy as they subdued the countries that we call the Mideast. As occupiers of Judea only Romans can authorize and implement the sentence of crucifixion (pp. 945, 946)." The Romans pull back from inflicting such a debasing penalty on a Roman citizen and, indeed, often spare the nobility and people of the higher social classes, while using the punishment regularly on slaves. Such savage death is in the mind of Paul as he writes of Jesus to the Philippians: He did not cling to equality to God but emptied himself, taking on the form of a slave . . . taking on the form of a man . . . he humbled himself and became obedient unto death, even to death on a cross (2:7–8).

Often representations of the crucifixion are as barely trustworthy as that depicting Simon of Cyrene's hefting the long part of the cross behind Jesus, shifting the weight forward and making it more, rather than less, difficult for Jesus to carry it. The common display of nails being driven through the hands of Jesus is physically impossible, as the hands would tear away under the weight of the body, and, where nails are used in these ancient times, they are often driven through a small wooden plaque placed against the wrist to fix the limb into place. We have no record of whether the feet of Jesus are nailed, although, in ancient practice, they are often affixed, again with a small slab of steadying wood, to the side of the cross.

Jesus later bids the doubting Thomas to examine his hands and his feet, to see the marks of the nails (Luke 24:39; John 20:25,27). Early commentators also mention the hands and the feet but scholars believe that they are making a spiritual, rather than an historical, connection with Psalm 22:17: They have pierced my hands and my feet. *The Hebrew word* yad *covers not only the hand but the entire forearm.*

The body of the person crucified is often supported by a small wooden shelf, serving as a partial seat and called a sedile. This gives some support, allowing minimal relief for breathing, thereby prolonging the life and suffering of the victim. Jesus dies relatively quickly, perhaps because he is so weakened by his earlier scourging and the exhausting journey to Calvary. Father Brown concludes that Jesus is not supported by this sedile nor by the footrest that is commonplace in the iconography of the crucifixion (pp. 949, 950).

Although something like a scaffold is often erected for mass executions and Jesus is sometimes portrayed as being crucified on one panel of such a device, with the wrongdoers hanging on either side of him, Tertullian compares Jesus' cross to a man standing with his arms stretched out. This, Father Brown observes, "has been a favorite of Christian art because Matthew 27:37 mentions that 'they put above his head the charge (p. 948).' "

In Mark this reads The King of the Jews; *in Matthew,* This Is Jesus, King of the Jews; *in Luke,* The King of the Jews, This Man; *and in John,* Jesus the Nazarean, the King of the Jews. *Jesus is mocked, again in a series of three, as he hangs beneath this inscription on the cross. The evangelists, borrowing and mixing from each other or a common source of story or memory, present these in slightly varying but strongly similar ways.*

The clinically observant physician Luke, as we have seen, makes a distinction about the crowd for, if some mock Jesus, many others are sympathetic to him. The rulers carry out a further humiliation, speaking of Jesus in the third person and mocking him to each other, as powerful men on the sidelines of someone else's woe do to this day. We hear their cackling laughs of ridicule as they mock his ability to save himself, Others he has saved, let him save himself! *(Mark 2, Matthew 2) Their laughter erupts like a congested gutter,* Come down from the cross . . .

They are safe, they have what they want, they can join their mockery with the claims Jesus makes and the charges they forge against him. The sour but self-satisfied mood of a deed long needed and finally done by men it makes into temporary and untrusting comrades—for which will turn his back with any ease on the other?—turns the space around the cross into that of a prison yard, inviting the catcall derision of the soldiers. If you are the King of the Jews, save yourself. *Power, betrayal, the roll of the dice, and cast your lot with the man who wins, that is the shrunken moral universe into which one of the wrongdoers crucified next to Jesus hurls his taunt,* Save yourself and us.

Who are these men who are crucified with Jesus?

And with him, Mark tells us, they crucify two bandits. Indeed, all the Gospel writers describe these men and place them at either side of Jesus. From early commentators flow elaboration and information about them, including a range of names for each. "All this," Father Brown observes, "goes beyond the Gospels, which mention them without explanation but without embarrassment that Jesus is being treated as one of several criminals (p. 969)." They are included "to illustrate the indignity with which the innocent Jesus was subjected (loc. cit.)." They are to take on important roles in the crucifixion, however, as one joins in the mockery with his challenge to Jesus. If you are so powerful, save yourself and save us, too.

The other crucified man, however, sympathizes with Jesus, affirming, along with many of the Jews in the crowd—as a Roman guard will an hour and more later, that he has done no wrong. Does Luke draw from some oral memory or other source not used by the other Gospel writers? Is it not possible, our guide asks, "to think of this as a Lucan theological creation," that is, an invention to expand his teaching about Jesus' mercy rather than a strictly historical account? Luke accomplishes many things, Brown concludes, by devel-

oping this story, including the presentation of the other wrongdoer as another impartial witness to Jesus' innocence "in a chain stretching from Pilate and Herod before Jesus' death to the centurion after his death (pp. 1001, 1002)." Jesus heals and saves throughout the drama of his seizure, trial, his carrying the cross to this place, and hanging, crucified, before our eyes.

# Now

Joseph knows that he has reached the place of the skull. It is October and he will soon abandon the chemotherapy whose help is too little and whose side-effect nausea is very great. Emptying himself, he turns over his authority to run the archdiocese to his assistant bishops, for he does not see this as something to be clung to. He knows in his being and bones, as a sailor does the deep secrets of the sea, that Death is no longer a vague shadow turning in at a distant lane but that he has entered the house and shed his cloak and is filled with Light rather than darkness, a friend come to call, as Joseph says, rather than an enemy come to conquer.

He speaks of death this way at a press conference he holds in a crowded room in the diocesan office building, a few steps from the hall in which, three years before, he meets the reporters, believing that the truth would make him free. He learns a new truth the day before, after what he believes is a routine checkup with Dr. Ellen Gaynor, *Your cancer has returned, in your liver, a year, perhaps.* Joseph is not unprepared but he knows now the small mockery of the term *cancer-free* that, until this moment, he uses to describe his condition and his confidence that he is making a recovery. This truth tells him that he is not free at all, that he has borne the cross in his back to this place, that his way of the cross is drawing to an end.

He decides to tell the truth to the city and the world by meeting with the reporters again. It is in the afternoon, live on television, in a space as crowded as the small hill of Golgotha, and Death is here, too. Joseph is straightforward in his announcement and speaks with such peace and joy that another kind of hush falls on the mostly young journalists staring at him in the glare of the lights. He speaks of death to these men and women who still feel immortal and for whom death is a vague specter who visits other people, never them. Joseph tells them the truth about the return of his cancer, investing them with the gift of his own peace and calm, taking questions, reading them the prayer of St. Francis that he carries in his pocket: *Lord, make me an instrument of your peace. . . .*

But it is October and he has been to Rome and suffered its bureaucratic rebuff, and he will carry the cross of his back as long as he can. Joseph's life moves into a groove of time out of time as everything slows down and he senses that his destiny is coming full upon him. The doctors speak to him of a year but he feels within himself that the cup of final suffering and death is being offered to him now. He tells me of his visit to Dr. Gaynor. *I told her that I have read my own situation accurately so far and now I have a new reading. I have entered a new phase of this illness. I can no longer attribute the fatigue to the chemotherapy. The disease has progressed. She agreed with me. The largest spot on my liver is now twice as large as it was six weeks ago, the smaller one is half again as big. You can probably hear it in my voice. I intend to take my calendar and strike off things and do only those for the good of the Church and the Church in Chicago. I want to finish the little book I am writing. . . .*

A solemn feeling wells out of a pause after he takes a breath. *You've crossed a threshold?* I ask. *Yes. . . .*

I felt pain in my chest and my arm on the trip to see her. These are secondary to the cancer. I know that I am reading this correctly.

His phone rings, it is one of the high priests, Cardinal Law, asking how he is. *I am fine, Bernie, fine* . . . He is offering genuine hospitality to the prelate who, as Joseph well knows, has done everything he can to diminish Joseph's position and influence in the Church, the prince who, to curry favor in the Roman court, immediately condemns Joseph's *Common Ground* initiative. Joseph thanks him for an event Bernie orchestrates to honor him in Boston, and to which, on a private plane, Joseph flies, as draining a passage as any he makes on a journey that is now coming rapidly to an end. *Yes, thank you, Bernie, and thank you for your prayers.* Joseph hangs up, smiles, one old friend to another, *You know you're the only one of my friends who understands how tiring it is for me to speak on the telephone.* He smiles, *Bernie and these others are going to kill me with these calls.*

Joseph finds a good thief on the skull-like grounds of the Joliet State Prison, from which a condemned man sends a message asking Joseph to visit him. On a broiling September day, he journeys to the prison, with its grim brick structures, from which catcalls fall on him—*Hey, you motherfuckin' priest, who are you, what are you here for?*—as he makes his way across the hard-packed prison yard dirt scored into crooked canyonlike rivulets by a century of rainstorms, toward the dilapidated one-story brick building in which the condemned man waits. We are a biblical triad, we three, Monsignor Kenneth Velo, Kevin Dowdle, and me, who accompany him but can only watch his visit to the prisoner through the small mesh inlaid window in the massive paint-chipped gray steel door to the corridor of holding cells reserved for the dead men walking. The prisoner's hands gesture through the bars, one hand touches and grips Joseph's arm as they talk, and he tells him of his life and how he kills people and now he is come to this last day. . . .

Joseph finds another companion on the cross, no wrongdoer in his sight, but crucified by cancer in the same autumn. Joseph speaks often with the hospitalized Steven Cook before, as Joseph tells me, he enters paradise after a short hard life. Joseph treasures a letter that Steven writes to him when he first learns of Joseph's cancer diagnosis: *I was shocked and unhappy to hear the news, I remembered how much I cried or sobbed in my car after leaving the oncologist's office knowing that I needed chemo, it is devastating and scary. I even found myself shedding a tear for you today. I am displeased that my actions caused so much heartache two years ago, now knowing that devastating news has come your way. . . . I've been dealing with my own mortality, chronic physical discomfort and the fear of the future (Will it hurt? How long do I have? Are there any good days left?) for several years now and if there is anything I can do to give you comfort or support I am ready, willing, and able. . . . Peace, Steven Cook.*

Joseph reaches that place to which he has been called, and toward which many routes, some blind alleys or dead ends, join beneath his feet as his last mile. He knows that he stands at the place of the skull, that he is soon to finish the work the Father has given him to do.

The TWELFTH STATION:
Jesus Dies on the Cross

Then

*The loud cry from the depths of the crucified Jesus carries across the
waters of the centuries to enter our own depths and opens us to the
darkness at the heart of this Mystery—his mystery, our mystery,
the mystery—the seed and flower of this instant in which Jesus can
express no ultimate triumph over death because he is overwhelmed by
his stark feeling of being abandoned by his Father.* My God, my
God, why have You forsaken me? *Although the sun is swallowed
by the Mystery at the sixth hour, that high Judean noon of raising
Jesus on the cross, this filter gives light enough for us to see that our
place is not that of spectators but as participants in this redemption
of us, just as we are, in the world, just as it is.*

Indeed, without the shadow that still stretches across the land as we reach the ninth hour, or three o'clock in the afternoon, we would not see that the Mystery cannot be divine unless it is first human. If Jesus takes away our sins, he first takes on our sorrows, if he has had no place on which to lay his head, we have had no place in which to store these sorrows, and he pours the vastness of our human loss into this two-hearted river of time and eternity. Here, as symbolic darkness descends, the temple veil is shredded and the earth cracks open with wonders. The dying Jesus is mocked, here, too, and drinks of the vinegary wine before he wails in desolation and dies. In this last cry uttered from the depth of his suffering—that is, in fact, the depth of our own suffering—Jesus reveals and ratifies his identification with all human travail. All this may be heard as Jesus cries out, "not in rage," Father Brown notes, "but in prayer (p. 1044)."

The Gospel accounts are composed as carefully as tapestries are sewn, with great central panels in which the words and actions are chosen not only to reveal the event but to evoke the scriptures that are being fulfilled before our eyes. So, as Jesus is offered vinegary wine, we hear the echo of Psalm 69:22, And they gave for my bread gall, and for my thirst they gave me to drink vinegar, *"words," as Father Brown notes, "describing how the just one is mocked by his enemies (p. 1059)."*

But Jesus' lonely shout is a lightning dagger that shears through the web of midday darkness and explodes on the skull's brow of Golgotha. Jesus invests this loud cry, or scream, as its fierceness is sometimes translated, with his understanding of everything human, giving voice to our trembling store of pain in an outcry that is not a plea for mercy for our sins but a plaint for all the rejection, hurt, and separation of all humans. He feels it all as he surrenders willingly to this moment, its last possibility of comfort scoured and skinned out by his Father's withdrawal from him—all the sorrows of time, all the bloodied hands gripping iron bars, all the arms bearing wasted and dying children, all the backs bent and scarred by unjust punishments, all the terrified eyes glimpsed as boxcar doors slide shut, all the sweet-faced youth stunned into blank staring death on muddy fields, all those taken down by heartbreak, all those crying against the sky for losses too great to bear or too small to name, all those whose gifts are never even opened, and all those denied even a taste of the battered, bittersweet glory of being human—for all these Jesus intones this lament in a desperate call from the cross that finishes his Father's work by braiding our sorrows into his own.

The death of Jesus occurs in the Gospels not only beneath the starless tent of darkness stretched taut above him hanging on the cross but to the rumbling and rupture of earthquake and whirlwind, to the Just rising from shattered tombs and, in the Temple, to the rending of the great sanctuary veil. We have tasted this vinegary wine before and seen this darkness fall at midday in Jeremiah (15:9) as a symbol of God's wrath and later as a sign of God's breaking his pact with his people. Such darkness in other Old Testament scenes is so thick that men must light their lamps to find their way. How are we to understand this orchestration of extravagant wonders around the death of Jesus? Does the long-dead psalmist offer Jesus the wine, do the dead shake away the earth crumbs as they rise, does the temple veil convulse and come apart? Do these things really take place? And, if they do not occur in any literal sense, what are we to make of them?

Such operatic language is commonplace not only in the Scriptures that are written in the languages of myth and poetry but also in history's long scroll in which heavenly signs are often associated with the birth or death of kings or other great figures. So Plutarch writes of the sun's fleeing on the death of Romulus and to this day we describe sunny days that are marred by loss or heartbreak as dark days and sing the Blues about them. We speak easily of the sparkling, sunny morning of September 11 as a dark day, knowing that we are telling a deeper emotional truth than may be found in the records of the *weather bureau. Desolation and darkness flap like shattered main-sails above that mystery of loss much as they do for the three hours that Jesus is on the cross to complete his Father's work and his own. We are not uncomfortable speaking of this invading darkness that lines this Mystery, for we feel it and locate ourselves less by instruments of measurement than by metaphor, that lighted but swaying bridge that bears our weight across this chasm of loss in a Mystery that is theological rather than historical.*

All human sorrow is compressed into the cry of Jesus that so resonates with desolation that Father Brown asks aloud what we wonder in silence: how are we to understand this shout, and how literally should we take it? "There is much to encourage us," he answers, "to take it very literally on the level of the evangelists' portrayal of Jesus (p. 1045)." Because we have all sipped from this same cup, we know the deadly taste of the rejection that ravages Jesus in this reprise of the passion narrative: "Jesus has been abandoned by his disciples and mocked by all who have come to the cross. Darkness has covered the earth; there is nothing that shows God acting on Jesus' side. How appropriate that Jesus feel forsaken! His 'Why?' is that of someone who has plumbed the depths of the abyss, and feels enveloped by the powers of darkness. . . . He is questioning the silence of the one whom he calls 'My God.' (p. 1046)."

Our guide notes that in no previous prayer does Jesus address God as God. He is always and ever Father, and Jesus prays as confidently as a son when, with no answer, he prays three times in the garden that he may be spared from passing through the hour, this herald of time's mystery just rising off the turn of the earth, or to be excused from drinking of the cup that is but one hand away from being passed to him (Matthew 26:39). And now, as Father Brown observes, "having drunk the dregs of the cup, Jesus screams out a final prayer. . . . Feeling forsaken as if he were not being heard, he no longer presumes to speak intimately to the All-Powerful as 'Father'

but employs the address common to all human beings, 'My God'
(ibid)."

*Jesus speaks in this human way, we may judge, so that we cannot
miss that he is speaking in the midst of his own agony for the agony
of all of us, that this last and terrible cry is wrenched from a heart
that comprehends all our hearts. Here Father Brown notes the parallel with Paul's evocation in his letter to the Hebrews of the harsh
terms and hard learning of Jesus' calling (4:14–16; 5:7–10). "While
many aspects of the Hebrews passage had echoes in the . . . Gethse-
mane prayer, there are other aspects that have resemblance to the
prayer on the cross . . . on which Jesus has learned even more fully
'obedience from the things he suffered' . . . here that he has made
'strong clamor,' and . . . here that he will be 'heard from (anxious)
fear' and made perfect (p. 1047)."*

*We find this same cup of commanding but unsettling truth wait-
ing for us in this light, mottled as that of the moon by passing clouds,
at the center of this Mystery. As Jesus turns away from the sponge
soaked with drugged wine that would siphon his pain off into a
glassy dream, we reject the honeyed cup raised above this scene by so
many preachers to sweeten it and dilute its brutal mystery. The literal
interpretation of his feeling forsaken is softened by some commentators so that it loses the son's anguish at his Father's absence. Others
transform terrible loss into "loving surrender" while still others claim
that if we accept the idea that Jesus fully experiences abandonment by
his Father, we deny his divinity. In the same vein, others claim that
any admission that Jesus could experience such severe alienation
would challenge the serene communion with his Father that Jesus
expresses at other times, as in John: "I am never alone because the
Father is with me (16:32–33)."*

*After reviewing these and other interpretations forged by those
who, fearing to deny Jesus his divinity, deny him his humanity
instead, Father Brown concludes that "I find no persuasive argument*

against attributing to the Jesus of Mark/Matthew the literal senti-
ment of feeling forsaken. . . . One should accept . . . literally . . . this
screamed protest against abandonment wrenched from an utterly for-
lorn Jesus who now is so isolated and estranged that he no longer uses
'Father' language but speaks as the humblest servant (p. 1051)."

It is not a cup of abstract suffering that is passed to Jesus at this
moment but one that runs over with our pains and our flaws, both
purged by the white heat of existence. The cup that Jesus drinks, is it
not the same cup from which we all drink? Is it not the cup of this
Mysterium Tremendum et Fascinans *of Jesus' rejecting the role*
of a king to take that of a servant? For what can this mean and
how could we miss that Jesus waives his royal state that he may
instead enter our own as the suffering servant who saves us from
our sins by sharing our sufferings? That is the theological center of
this Passion Play that is no play. Only with the threads vivid and
wondrous could the evangelists suture together the great tapestry of
this profoundly human event. Let the sky darken and the tombs fall
open like the jaws of the dead; let this wild sirocco sweep across the
land, this sharp and savage wind so well known to us that it bites
our faces as it rips the temple veil asunder, this invisible wind, the
tempest of our every hazard and misfortune that rages as Jesus
breathes out his spirit and completes the work his Father has given
him to do.

 I COMMEND MY SPIRIT

As Jesus speaks his final words, Father, into Your hands I commend
my spirit, other phrases float up out of the deep of the Scriptures—the
chief priests seeking to lay their hands on Jesus (Luke 20:19) and
Jesus' own prophecy that the Son of Man would be given over into

the hands *of sinful men (Luke 9:44). Now Jesus gives his spirit into
the* hands *of the Father. We must know what this* spirit *means to
enter this slit in time and to enter our own wounds. Jesus is not giving a part of himself, a soul superior to the body, to the Father.
Rather, as Father Brown tells us, spirit signifies "all that he is and has
(p. 1068). Spirit," he continues, "is not simply a partial component of
the human being (as in 'soul' and body); it is the living self or life
power that goes beyond death* (ibid). *"Jesus is healing us of the divi-
sion of personality into warring elements of soul and body that, pro-
claimed by high priests, has caused so much suffering for humanity. If
this is only a portion of human suffering, it is great enough and is
encompassed in Jesus' surrender of self to the Father.*

Spirit *here "goes beyond the usual anthropological definitions," as
Father Brown observes, for Jesus is not only conceived of the Spirit,
whose symbol appears at his baptism in the waters of the Jordan, but
preaches across Judea in the power of the Spirit (Luke 4:14) and, as
he places his spirit in the Father's hands, "he is bringing round to its
place of origin his life and mission* (ibid). *"*

 ## THE LAMB OF GOD

*The evangelist John, as we have learned, emphasizes Jesus' remaining
in control of his life, his suffering, and his death. When Jesus says "I
thirst," therefore, he fulfills the prophecies that are realized in his own
life and mission as John explains,* "in order that the scriptures be
fulfilled, *he says 'I thirst.'"* John *describes the vinegary wine being
offered not on a spear or pole but on hyssop to echo Exodus 12:22
"which specifies that hyssop should be used to sprinkle the blood of the
paschal lamb on the doorposts of the Israelite homes. . . . Jesus is
judged at noon, the very hour when the slaughter of lambs for the*

Passover begins (pp. 1076, 1077)." Behold, John writes, this is the Lamb of God.

So, too, John, an eyewitness, records Jesus as saying, after he drinks the vinegary wine, "It is finished," revealing the same Jesus who says that he will drink the cup the Father gives him (John 18:11) understanding that he thereby finishes the work the Father gives him to do. As Father Brown summarizes this dazzling symbolism, "When Jesus drinks the wine from the sponge put on hyssop, *symbolically he is playing the scriptural role of the paschal lamb predicted at the beginning of his career, and so he has finished the commitment made when the Word become flesh. . . . His death becomes a deliberate decision that all is now finished, taken by one who is in control (p. 1077, 1078)."*

 ## THE DEATH OF JESUS

Mark and Luke, we learn, employ a simple description—the Greek ekpnein, *"to breathe out"—a term that resonates in our own usage of "to expire." Father Brown tells us that Jesus "let out the life force with his last breath" and that the contrived interpretations that he expels a demon with his last breath are fanciful. So, too, the Docetism, as it is called, that posits that we witness not the death of the real person of Jesus, a spiritual being who departs, but only the appearance of his body, diminishes the mystery by denying him his humanity. Jesus gives up his spirit, even as we do, and this Passion Play, as we note, is no play. This central aspect of the Mystery involves his taking on our deaths as well as our sins.*

Father Brown suggests that as Jesus bows his head before he goes to the Father, he is not surrendering to his suffering but is directing his spirit to those grouped by the cross. This bow is not theatrical but

136

it is dramatic, for Jesus is gazing at those human beings closest to him to give these sorrowing followers—and our surrogates—his spirit. "What more fitting," Father Brown observes, "than that those who did not go away when Jesus was arrested . . . but assembled at the cross, should be the first to receive" his spirit (p. 1082). How fitting, we may say, that, as Jesus bows his head to see better those he loves as he breathes his spirit on them, he sees all the men and women of all time, whom he also loves and whose suffering he takes unto himself as he gives them his spirit. This Mysterium Tremendum *is not about appearances, or the abstract transactions of distant gods, a breath that wafts into galaxies beyond our imagining. Jesus lowers his head to us, he looks into our eyes, for we are the subjects and the objects of the work his Father has given him to do. It is only as he breathes his spirit into our lives, brimming more with sorrows than sins, that he can say "It is finished."*

And so Father Brown concludes that the descriptions of Jesus' "being taken up" are theological in purpose and that they signify the "understanding that after his death Jesus had passed out of time (p. 1081)," out of that field in which we and our sorrows dwell together.

Now

Joseph is also finishing the work the Father gives to him as a son and now, as November steals the light, he is raised on the cross and the center of Chicago is no longer found at any intersection of famous streets, or in some finely paneled high-rise of financial or political power. If Chicago's center is now easily found in Joseph so, too, is its heart. The people who line the way of the final months of his life now watch silently as he reaches the summit of his own Calvary in his own residence, whose century-old brick walls are made radiant by Joseph, luminous, dying within them.

The city's ordinary people, unlike the kings finding their way to the manger, are guided not by a star signaling from the chill arena of the sky but by the soft glow of the old residence, in which those who love Joseph seem to glide through the hush that heralds death to perform their last services for the man who is also the center of their lives. If Joseph's mother is not there but in a nearby nursing home, still she senses, as we shall learn, what is taking place, what is happening to her only son. The other women are also there: Elaine, his sister, yes, and "Tanchie," Octavia Misoman, the secretary who follows him, as the women of Galilee do Jesus, through every town in which he preaches, finally entering Chicago with him on that Palm Sunday of his arrival as archbishop in 1982, and near him now, fourteen years and fourteen stations later.

There, too, stands his nun-doctor, cancer specialist Ellen Gaynor, who, not many days before this near-to-final one, shakes her head gently, *No*, she answers as Joseph calmly asks, *Will I be alive next week?* Joseph does not flinch, for he seems in control of his own dying, waving the specter down, neutralizing its threat, *You may land anytime now, I have been expecting you.* Joseph is at peace, *I will know*, he tells me a day after he receives his death sentence, *when death is here because Dr. Gaynor tells me that I will feel a kind of fatigue that I have never felt before.*

Sister Lucia is there as well, born in the same year as Joseph and, if he is a child of the misfortunes of South Carolina of the Great Depression, she is a child of the tragedy of Poland in the act-one Nazi blitzkrieg of World War II. She makes her way from camp to camp, deep into Siberia and out again, and around the world to discover that all her journeys lead to one special calling as a nun—to be both Martha and Mary in running his house and in caring for Joseph. These women find that Joseph is at the center of their lives, that he makes no secret entry and, if he takes nothing, yet he receives with a graciousness that binds them completely to him, this extraordinary man who takes possession of their hearts as gently as the first snowfall impounds the city. They are transformed by him, for they have never known, nor could they dream they would know, a man so truly a man and yet so unlike almost every other man.

The disciples Joseph loves are there as well, Kenneth Velo and Scott Donahue, each called away from their nets at other diocesan jobs to follow him and to find in his company and in his service—if it can be called that, so joyfully do they give themselves to it—finding a life around him so filled that time itself cannot betray its wonder. Not until now as they realize that they are keeping vigil for Joseph as he sheds the constraints of time as easily and unaffectedly as he removes his crimson robes at the end of a long day, yes, they know that night is falling on a man unafraid of the dark, and that, of his own will and without complaint, he is laying down his life, he is finishing his Father's work; that he is letting the strappings of time fall away as he enters the eternal not as a stranger but as one who already breathes its pure air.

Kenneth Velo brings him the completed manuscript of *The Gift of Peace* into which Joseph pours his last energies with a young editor, Jeremy Langford, who learns, as so many others do, that as you come close to Joseph you find that, in friendship and intimacy, he does not manipulate others into false unquestioning allegiance or keep them at a cool and formal distance, he is just there, fully and easily himself. You can come closer to Joseph without fearing that you will be lost.

Small wonder that people find themselves and their lives changing because they are close to Joseph. Every person who enters this residence during these last days receives the spirit from Joseph, yes, and the gift of peace, too, as his head bobs under the pressure of the fatigue that is invading him. Everyone feels that Joseph commissions them to carry his spirit into the world as he finishes his Father's work.

Still, friends call and some come and, as the burden of speaking becomes too great, he pulls himself together to listen. On Saturday, the retired San Francisco archbishop John Quinn—a close colleague in Joseph's work to strengthen the National Conference of Bishops as an effective collegial body—comes to see him but, seeing how valiantly Joseph struggles to push aside the hand of weariness that grips him, stays for only a quarter of an hour. That evening, Joseph goes to the chapel with his sister Elaine to attend Mass to be offered by Kenneth Velo, but he cannot hold himself erect in his chair and must yield to the forces that infiltrate his body and all but neutralize his strong will to maintain control to the very end. Kenneth calls others, including me and my wife, to tell them that the Mass is called off, it is too much for the Cardinal on this day when darkness comes in the afternoon.

On Sunday, Roger Cardinal Mahony of Los Angeles stops off to see Joseph on his way to the annual bishops' meeting in Washington, D.C. Joseph, lying exhausted on a sofa, asks him to be the principal celebrant at his funeral Mass. Mahony, alone of the other high priest American cardinals, stands with Joseph in the Common Ground proposal that Boston's Bernard Cardinal Law and Washington, D.C.'s James Hickey attack as quickly and as loudly as they can, and Joseph knows that their purpose is to guarantee that their voices are heard and approved of by the Pope. Their voices echo those of earlier high priests who complain of what Jesus teaches so openly in the Temple and that he must be brought down for it. It is stunning, through this long and subdued weekend, to watch these men accept their roles as their destinies, as knowing and unknowing of what they are doing as those Jesus forgives from the cross and Joseph does from his bed in this Passion Play that is moving so rapidly to its conclusion.

Bishop Raymond Goedert, the Vicar General of the archdiocese who lives in the residence, prepares to leave for the bishops' meeting. Joseph gestures to him, *Could you wait for a few moments?* and makes his way against the current of his fatigue to the desk in the office in his suite of rooms. He takes out a sheet of stationery and begins to write in blue ink on the paper. He cannot control the pen and his script that always flows as smoothly as a great river now washes against submerged wrecks and broken bridges that shatter its rhythm and trim. He crumples one piece of paper and starts again but pauses, lays his fatigue-infected arms on the desk, takes a breath, begins again a last letter, haltingly, carefully, to bid goodbye to his brother bishops. *Dear Bishop Pilla, I had every hope of attending the bishops' meeting in Washington. Unfortunately, my rapidly deteriorating health will not make it possible. Please extend my regards to the bishops. Assure them of my prayers and best wishes. I have been a member of our Episcopal Conference for thirty years. It is a wonderful structure of Episcopal Communion. I pray that the work of the Committee on Mission and Structure will refine the conference's work and encourage many bishops to participate in it. Please, Bishop Pilla, assure all the bishops of my prayers and love. My only request of them is that they pray that God will give me the strength and grace I need each day. May God bless you all. Peace and love, Joseph.*

It is finished. He gives it to Bishop Goedert to bear as his last words to the Conference to which he always gives his best energies and to which he now gives his last. He has written to attempt to head off what he knows the high priests have put into motion, a downgrading of the bishops' conference that surrenders to Rome the rights the bishops possess by their ordination and by the theology that endorses the teaching authority of the bishops in each country. They do gut the conference within a few years, spreading their own authority on the fire as an offering to please the Pope and Roman officials. The effort, made more difficult because Joseph knows that it is a losing one, empties him. He moves slowly away from the desk and lowers himself carefully onto the bed that is more cross than comfort for him.

Sister Lucia brings him some 7-Up in a glass with a bent straw. *The doctor says you should drink this.* Joseph can barely speak now but he accepts this counterpart of the vinegary wine and tries, as he does every day of his life, to do his duty, to do what is expected of him. Elaine watches, remembering Joseph as a little boy and a big brother, Joseph, always dutiful, always there, giving of himself, he has given almost everything now.

Throughout the residence, those who love him most, priests like Kenneth Velo and Scott Donahue, are lost in memory as well, for they are family to Joseph, his beloved sons who are with him in times of joy, serving Joseph, living in his circle, joking with him, celebrating feasts, especially Christmas, the one he loves best, with a tree trimming party, and being with him in bad times, such as the false accusation of sex abuse, that land-mine whose explosion on a November afternoon just three years before still sounds within them, and they recall the tumbling images of that time in which they have a privileged view of his goodness and his supple strength, let no man think there is no steel beneath that gentleness, in adversity. With them is Kevin Dowdle, a young and successful trader in the wild Chicago pits, who becomes a member of the household, carrying out his share of tasks in the blessed intimacy of this old residence. He is everywhere that anyone needs him during these days, tears streaming down his handsome black Irishman's face.

Speaking of these young priest to me a few months before, Joseph says *I am not going to leave them orphans, I am not going to leave them to figure everything out when I die.* He spends time in the last months of his life making arrangements for his funeral and burial, for ongoing care for his mother, clearing up all the details that he can, including the distribution of the Lladro porcelain choirboys he selects as his Christmas gifts to his closest friends. On the plane back from his trip to Rome in September, he asks Kenneth Velo to preach at the Mass of the Resurrection that will be his funeral. As tears fill Kenneth's eyes, Joseph touches his hand to his arm, speaks softly, *I have shed tears of my own.* Scott Donahue accompanies him earlier in the summer on his last trip to the town from which his parents came and where many cousins still live just below the Dolomite Mountains in Northern Italy. Scottie, as everyone calls him, is at Joseph's side at Philadelphia's St. Charles Seminary on the last day of 1994 as Joseph reconciles with his accuser, Steven Cook, anointing him with the sacrament of the sick before celebrating Mass for him in the chapel there. Scottie insists, six months later, that Joseph make and keep a doctor's appointment when the first minor symptoms of his cancer appear. Kenneth and Scottie are with Joseph through the surgery, the recovery, and the arc of convalescence that snaps a year later as Ellen Gaynor tells him after what Joseph presumes is a routine checkup that his cancer has returned.

They witness in the succeeding months the way Joseph gives himself to cancer patients on his own visits to the Loyola Hospital Cancer Center and how, at the same desk where he labors to write his farewell to his brother bishops, he writes hundreds of notes to the cancer patients for whom he is not the Cardinal-Archbishop of Chicago as much as he is their pastor. Kenneth thinks now of a familiar sight, Joseph on the telephone, speaking to someone become brother or sister to him in suffering, taking on their suffering, making it his own.

There is a stream of visitors, but by Monday afternoon Joseph can barely speak and Mass is offered in his room as he can no longer make it downstairs. His blood pressure drops and Sister Lucia hears the doctor say that he cannot live long, a day perhaps, or two at the most. Joseph can no longer move and can focus for only brief moments. He is surrounded by those who love him, his beloved disciples and the women who care for him, each thinking of other times and other days and the sorrow sharpened on the edges of the calendar pages that, like the autumn leaves, are almost all fallen away now.

Images arise from nowhere. There is Joseph on his last public appearance on October 29, standing patiently on a balcony above the crowd at the renaming of the Loyola Center as the Joseph L. Bernardin Cancer Center. The university president reads a long citation as Joseph, pale as the walls, struggles to remain erect—*Look at him!*—as he gazes down at the applauding crowd and cannot quite form a smile as he turns away toward the banquet that is to be held in an adjacent tent already rain-soaked and billowing like the canvas on a storm-doomed sailing vessel. The signs on this night with no stars are apocalyptic and, just before the banquet begins, one side of the tent is rent in two and flaps loose to welcome the tempest into this canvas temple.

At the residence, a guard stands by, a Chicago policeman in plainclothes who is detailed to the house, who knows from years of watching him that Joseph is a good and just man. Bishop Goedert returns immediately from delivering Joseph's letter to the bishops in Washington to be present as Joseph enters the final hours of his life.

On the last full day, the President calls and so does the Pope, but Joseph can only listen as they speak to him. He whispers *Thank you* to the Pope, the last words Kenneth Velo hears him utter. But it is far into the bitter cold darkness, long after the sun has departed and hours before it rises again that Joseph breathes his last, yielding up the spirit that he has long since given to the loved ones around his bed and to the city and the world beyond. It is finished. He completes the work the Father gave him to do.

T͟H͟E͟ THIR͟EENTH STATI⦿N:
The Body of Jesus Is Taken Down from the Cross

 Then

Jewish law and custom insist that the bodies of those crucified are to be taken down and buried before the sun sets. The Romans advertise their brutality by allowing corpses, decaying and attacked by carrion, to hang in public sight for uncertain periods of time. It is afternoon and, although the guards break the legs of the wrongdoers on either side of Jesus to hasten their deaths, they see that Jesus is already dead and, although they spare his body this indignity, one of the soldiers pierces his side and, almost as if we are witnesses, we testify to what we have heard all our lives, that blood and water flow from this wound.

It is silent around the crosses except for the low voices of the guards as they unwittingly fulfill other prophecies by making a game of chance out of who shall have the garment, seamless in tradition, that is removed from Jesus as he is prepared for crucifixion. Dice are unlikely, despite the long tradition of their clacking sound as they are rolled on the stony ground to settle the matter. More likely, these soldiers make their wager by trying to guess, as children do, how many fingers the other throws behind his back. And so the garment, which is to become legendary, is won and handed off and the accustomed resolution of who shall get the leftovers of crucifixion is completed. It is routine, over quickly, who can pay much heed to these huddled soldiers and their low voices and laughter?

After the intensity of the long day, the crowd, even though it counts many sympathizers in its number, fragments, as crowds do after great events, and moves away sluggishly. As the sun releases its grasp on the spring sky, those who love and follow Jesus are filled with mourning and uncertainty about how to care for him. His body is in the custody of the soldiers and under the control of the ambivalent procurator, Pilate, who feels clear of the blood that will splatter down the steps of the generations of those to whom he consigned the innocent young King of the Jews. Now comes Joseph into our view, identified by all the evangelists as from Arimathea, a site outside Galilee and not easily found, the counterfigure to Pilate, with whom he is linked in history's memory. Finding the procurator's eyes, he asks for permission to claim the body of Jesus and to bury it in a place which we also know well, in a nearby garden, as it is called, in a new tomb, belonging to this man from Arimathea, cut out of the rock.

Joseph is described as a "council member," for Mark is eager for us to know (15:43) that he is a member of the Sanhedrin, despite the fact, as Father Brown notes, that "previously Mark has portrayed all the Sanhedrists as having sought testimony against Jesus in order to put him to death (14:55) and as having given him over to Pilate (p. 1214)." Mark introduces Joseph as a man we would not expect to be moved at or concerned by the death of Jesus. But the evangelist fur-

ther describes him as "a man awaiting the Kingdom of God." Joseph's symbolic testimony is joined to that of the centurion as a spontaneous expression of surprising sympathy for Jesus. He steps forward to ask permission from Pilate to bury the body of the man condemned and crucified by the Sanhedrin as one guilty of blasphemy. "Joseph's concern," our teacher notes, is "perfectly consistent with Jewish piety" that would not, despite its concerns about defilement by the dead, allow a corpse to go unburied in such circumstances (p. 1216).

Nonetheless, it takes courage for even a Jew as presumably pious as Joseph to approach the Roman governor for permission to recover and bury the body. He could easily be singled out and condemned as a follower of Jesus, yet it seems clear that he enters from stage left, by himself, a wealthy and comfortable man with no relationship to those men and women who attend Jesus during his passion and death. And so the scene is set and Pilate steps back onto the stage to listen briefly to Joseph. He reacts with surprise, signals for a centurion. Is it true that this Jesus is already dead? The centurion confirms it and who can say what thoughts or feelings are touched off in Pilate, does he sense that, despite his efforts to keep clear of this matter, he will never be free of it?

Pilate nods, orders that the body "be given up" to Joseph, perhaps the procurator is finally fully separated from the unsettling events of the day (Matthew 27:58). Pilate does not look back as he steps into history, and even though he turns one way and Joseph of Arimathea another, they enter the field of legend as comrades at arms. If Pilate is thought to brood like Hamlet and become a Christian later and Joseph is memorialized as a secret follower of Jesus, they live still under these uncertain identities in our common imagination. Both are the subjects of novels and plays and Joseph is even cast by William Blake in his great poem "Jerusalem" as Jesus' rich uncle who brings him as a boy on a merchant's tour to gaze on the broad fields and the satanic mills of England. "Who," Father Brown asks, "could have

*foreseen such a career (in literature but, alas, not in fact)...
(p. 1234)?" Joseph is a mysterious actor in a greater Mystery, that of
the storm-swept world just as it is, a symbol at least, along with
Pilate, of the large faults and the small but saving nobility that wash
through the human condition.*

*But we are not done with meeting supporting players in our Pas-
sion Play. Only in John do we meet Nicodemus, described as having
come first to Jesus at night, as if fearing to be identified as a follower.
John writes of him as belonging to the realm of darkness before he
comes to the light of the world (8:12, 9:5). Nicodemus steps assuredly
into this story to assist Joseph in burying the body of Jesus. This is by
no means an anonymous burial and this is no unmarked grave.
Nicodemus provides a hundred-pound weight of spices that suggest,
as Brown tells us, "messianic abundance," so that Jesus is to be accorded
"a burial fit for a king (pp. 1260, 1261)." Nicodemus is also a member of the Sanhedrin and John's purpose is to show how he and Joseph
are transformed through the victory of Jesus on the cross (p. 1267).
Once hesitant to commit themselves to Jesus in the open, they now
give glory to God publicly as Joseph makes his own burial place avail-
able and Nicodemus purchases enough spices to fill it to overflowing.
John presents these men as responding to Jesus as the victor on the
cross, thereby fulfilling what Jesus says earlier: "When I am lifted up,
I shall draw all to myself (12:31–34)."*

 # Now

The women who are with Joseph Bernardin in his work are nearby as he finishes the labors that God gives him to do. Joseph dies in the bitter cold middle of the night with the disciples who love him at his bedside. Is Matthew Lamb the Joseph of Arimathea as he prepares to receive Joseph's body at his North Side funeral home? And is Kevin Dowdle our Nicodemus, ready to give or do anything to assist Joseph in life and to bear him fittingly to his resting place? Is not Joseph's victory from his cross of suffering one that draws all to himself and through him to the Lord, learning that, beyond all his achievements and honors, his work is to live again the life of Jesus and to bring it to an end by embracing those who suffer far more than they sin: It is finished, yes, but as he empties himself, he is already drawing all through himself to Jesus.

The news of Joseph's death spreads quickly across the still-sleeping city so that long before dawn television interviewers are waiting at bus stops and subway stations to put their questions to those just beginning the business of their day. *Have you heard the news? Yes,* they answer, *What do you think of him? A saint,* they respond without hesitation. As in the residence itself, Chicago begins preparations to bury the cardinal it loves so deeply. How typical and yet how fitting that a great gentleness should settle on this rough-and-tumble city, that everyone who is interviewed says the same thing. *Yes, we are sad but we know that he is in Heaven.*

Inside the house, so suddenly empty, so suddenly filled with daylight as the shades are raised and the blinds are opened and bustle returns to this zone fully occupied by sadness, yet filled with friends and disciples preparing for the funeral that is to take place in the next week. Kenneth Velo opens the side drawer in the desk at which Joseph, chief shepherd of Chicago's cancer victims, writes hundreds of notes of prayer and encouragement. He pauses, remembering Joseph's saying softly that this pastoral work is what he loves to do. Joseph, embracing human sorrow, corresponds or speaks on the phone during his last autumn with more than six hundred men, women, and children suffering serious illness.

Kenneth pulls himself back to the work at hand and opens the lower right-hand drawer. It is filled with manila folders, each prepared and labeled in advance by Joseph, that contain his instructions on most of the matters about which Kenneth and Scottie and others must now make decisions. *I will not leave them orphans.*

And Kenneth and Scottie and other close disciples address the many details of the Mass of the Resurrection that is to be offered, with Cardinal Mahony as principal celebrant, at Holy Name Cathedral on State Street several blocks south of the residence. Kenneth takes time from these many demands to prepare to carry out the last commission Joseph gives him, to preach at this Mass that is to be attended by all the high-priest cardinals, including those who have been openly critical of Joseph, by Joseph's family, including some cousins from Italy, by most of the country's bishops, and by hundreds of laypeople to be seated in pews marked off simply for *Friends.* It is to be watched by millions on CNN, the station that is yet to explain how it involved itself in an exclusive deal with the lawyer who accuses Joseph, on flimsy evidence he boasts about on CNN, of sexually abusing Steven Cook. The lawyer's role is now clear as an unknowing instrument of the Father in initiating Joseph's three-year public ministry.

The loyal women continue to serve Joseph in these labors—for he wants the residence, Sister Lucia knows, sparkling clean for visitors—and there are meals to make and doors to open and telephones to answer almost without a stop. Outside, the bobbing white television cranes stand like grounded and graceless shorebirds, angling to see who is coming and going by the front and side doors of the residence. Nearby neighbors and others from afar begin to heap candles and flowers and simple messages of affection on the steps on the State Street side of the residence as silence settles as peacefully as a first snowfall inside its walls. The man who fills the house with his gentle goodness seems gone and not gone, a victor from his cross, still present among those who live and work there.

Yet we find counterparts to the soldiers who gamble for possession of the seamless robe of Jesus in those who vie now to take something from Joseph in death after mocking him in life. They might as well throw fingers behind their backs as they compete to see who may seize Joseph's seamless garment, the name given to his 1989 proposal of a Unified Ethic of Life under which he lists not just abortion but all the issues in which the value and meaning of human life are at risk in American society. Joseph wishes to broaden and transform the Pro-Life program of the country's bishops so that it cannot be dismissed as a single issue concern and, while many accept and endorse this as a step that can only yield gain, many others, including the familiar high priest ecclesiastics, attack him and his proposals, accusing him of "being soft" on abortion. While he lies dying within the residence, a small group of extreme protestors outside pickets Joseph and mocks his seamless garment of Pro-Life issues.

His body is just being borne out of the residence on the shoulders of those he loves when other critics begin to claw at the seamless garment, to make their wagers as to which faction should possess and divide it. In smaller ways, too, men, for their own purposes, are making claims on nonexistent friendships with Joseph or telling of how they are important influences in his life. He smiles, I think, as in eternity he hears these familiar false voices echoing through the long halls of time. In New York, a media-savvy rabbi claims that he possesses a crimson cardinal's cincture that Joseph removes, folds, and hands to him as a blessing on his proposed search for certain important religious scrolls. Joseph's friends smile at the thought that he, so modest and understated, would ever make such a theatrical gesture. Still, the fingers are being thrown everywhere by men anxious to have a piece of his garment as a talisman, a ticket of approval or an upgrade in their public relations stature. But Joseph wears his seamless garment into eternity, and downtown, Father Jack Wall, pastor of old St. Patrick's, looks down from the ABC television studios at the State-Lake Theater where the marquee reads *Joseph and His Technicolor Dreamcoat*. He smiles, speaks softly, *Joseph really does have his technicolor dreamcoat now.*

I will not leave them orphans. Everyone close to Joseph understands exactly what he wants now, they can hear his voice, see his approving smile and they move as in a dream of gratitude and sorrow preparing for the moment when Joseph's body will be brought back to the residence to lie in state in the small chapel so that Joseph's family and a small group of his close friends may keep brief vigil with him before it is brought down State Street to Holy Name Cathedral where the women who love and serve him—Elaine and Tanchie, Sister Lucia and chief of staff Sister Brian Costello—will bear the liturgical white veil and place it on the catafalque in the sanctuary and later spread it on his coffin for the funeral Mass.

The hearse turns slowly into the curving drive that leads under the old-fashioned port cochere under which carriages rattled a hundred years before. The papal flag snaps in the chill wind as the casket is removed and a group of close friends carry it up the steep front steps and through the great oak-trimmed doorway and to the small private chapel just to the right. The coffin is opened and Joseph's sister Elaine and her husband, Jim, enter with their children for a period of family visitation. Then the extended family of close friends, perhaps thirty or so, joins them for a silent peaceful moment of prayer less for Joseph than with Joseph. Joseph is back home with the gift of peace for everyone.

An hour later, as the members of the family and close friends whisper stories of special moments with Joseph, a courier delivers an advance edition of the next issue of *Newsweek* with Joseph's picture on the cover and inside an essay by Kenneth Woodward about Joseph's last great mission: to teach America, embattled with its own mortality, how to die. The sadness is dispersed in the genial mood, Joseph's mood, that radiates throughout the rooms as if from the thousand smiles this extended family has witnessed on his face under this same roof, beneath their own roofs, too, or in ballrooms, boardrooms, and gatherings of the principalities and the powers, the thrones and dominations of the Chicago elite. Among these close friends are such influential figures as lawyer Philip Corboy and his wife, Library Commissioner Mary Dempsey, along with Ellen and Jim O'Connor, who heads Commonwealth Edison. But there, too, are Ignacia Capone, whose Italian cooking Joseph savors, and Zita Asay, who cares for Joseph's mother, women unknown to the public but well known to Joseph. Joseph is the same in all these settings and all these relationships, for, as his friends remark, there is never any difference between the public and the private Joseph, he is the same, ever a man in full to all. Stories are traded to gentle laughter, but of all these stories, let us listen to only one, that of a Christmas season in which Joseph asks for Campari in every house he visits, and how his friends lay in a supply for the next year and he never asks for it again, they all have nearly full bottles on hand, they smile and feel the pressure of tears, and know that Joseph, smiling gently, is truly present among them.

This visitation lasts but a few hours and soon Joseph's family and his extended family are ushered into cars, Joseph's body is placed again in the hearse, and the cavalcade turns onto State Street for the slow procession to the cathedral. Father Donahue arranges for parishioners, carrying handbells, to line the first great block of the famous old street. The hearse and cars head under pale sunshine on the updraft of these ringing bells, seeing Joseph off in a joyous cascade of sound, brightening the spirits of the friends accompanying him past waving children and wonder-struck adults, saluting policemen standing crisply at attention and cement-splattered construction workers laying down their tools to cross themselves, to the limestone cathedral to which hundreds of thousands of Chicagoans come throughout the bitter North Pole night to bid farewell to the holy man who was their archbishop.

The FOUREENTH STATION:
Jesus Is Laid in the Tomb

 Then

In narrating the burial of Jesus, the writers of the Gospels reveal their theological intentions. In these we always discover the spiritual meaning that transcends the small details or apparent inconsistencies that some obsessive yet ingenious scholars take for concrete history and try to harmonize, sometimes making rough the smooth path of the story.

So Father Brown, reflecting on the oral history of these events on which the writers depend, identifies what he terms a "pre-Gospel" narrative. He reminds us that "The burial by Joseph in itself really does no more than conclude the crucifixion, but the presence of other or secondary figure(s) allows other functions (p. 1235)." Raising this lantern above the swift actions after Jesus is dead and his body given to Joseph of Arimathea, we can see better the role of the women who stay close to Jesus throughout his life, are nearby at the crucifixion, witness his burial, and return to find the stone with which the Pharisees sealed the burial site is rolled away and that the tomb is empty.

Thus, for Mark, "the burial is a connective between the death of Jesus and the narrative of the tomb left empty by the resurrection of Jesus, with Joseph pointing back to what has happened and the women pointing forward to what will happen (loc. cit.)." Both Mark and Luke end with the women of Galilee, who have a privileged view of Jesus' three-year public life and stand near the cross during his agony; they are also eyewitnesses to his burial. This is carried out without delay as, according to Jewish law, it must be done before the approaching sunset.

How much of this familiar account of Jesus' being laid in the tomb is theological and how much of it may be regarded as fact? Father Brown answers in this way: "That Jesus was buried is historically certain. That Jewish sensitivity would have wanted this done before the oncoming Sabbath . . . is also certain. . . . That the burial is done by Joseph of Arimathea is very probable. . . . There is nothing in the basic pre-Gospel account of Jesus' burial by Joseph that could not plausibly be deemed historical (pp. 1240, 1241)."

In locating this tomb Brown notes that "A Joseph who was not a disciple would not have taken the trouble nor have had the time before the Sabbath to carry the crucified . . . body far away, consequently the tomb was (factually or plausibly) near Golgotha (p. 1271)." The presence of the women at the burial is presumed, because the Gospel accounts of their coming to the tomb early in the morning to discover that it is empty indicate a return rather than a first visit. Indeed, these women link the great moments of the narrative together.

In pre-Gospel memory, we see these women at Golgotha, first at a distance, then near the cross and the following morning, as they come to the tomb with spices and myrrh to care for the body of Jesus. These women make the long journey from Galilee with Jesus and, as the men disappear from the Gospel narratives, they remain in our view to follow after Joseph of Arimathea (Luke 23:25) so that they not only see the tomb but also "how the body of Jesus was placed therein (Brown, p. 1257)." They observe that it is wrapped in a cloth but that it is not anointed and "that is why they did not stay at the tomb but 'returned' to make preparations for the anointing (loc. cit.)." These women go unnamed at first, but those who come to the tomb to discover that Jesus is risen are identified as Mary Magdalene, Mary, perhaps the mother of James and Joses, and another woman, identified by some as Salome (cf. Brown, Discussion, p. 1277). What seems the end in burial in the tomb, then, is actually the beginning as Jesus triumphs over suffering and death and these women joyfully bring the news to the men closest to Jesus that the once-sealed tomb is empty, that Jesus is free of the bonds of death. Soon afterward, Jesus appears to the eleven disciples on a mountain in Galilee and sends them forth on their mission to teach all nations. The story, with its minor overlaps and uncertainties, with its angels and its wonders, is fundamentally that of the Resurrection on whose hope the Christian community establishes its foundations.

Now

The captains and the kings of American political life come to Chicago for the Mass of Resurrection and Joseph's being laid in the tomb in the Catholic cemetery a dozen miles and more due west from downtown Chicago. Vice President Al Gore and his wife, Tipper, represent the President and several high-ranking officials, including White House Chief of Staff Leon Panetta and several cabinet members, are seated in the front row. Nearby is Chicago's mayor, Richard M. Daley, and his wife, Maggie, and other state and municipal officials. But most of the pews are set aside, as Joseph plans it, for the thousand men and women known simply as *Friends*. They will be in the procession, limited to one hundred cars, that follows the hearse to the cemetery.

The high priests are here, too, all the cardinals, including Law, who is already making moves on the ecclesiastical chessboard to bring a bishop of his choosing into Chicago to succeed Joseph. He cannot see or imagine how all the power he has amassed will be challenged a few years later by the sex abuse scandal that Joseph warns him and his fellow bishops about in vain. For the moment, he controls the official Church in America and the bishops and abbots clustered about him recognize that, even though a personal representative of the Pope is present, Law is the master come to bury the man who makes himself into a servant to live again the life of Jesus before the people of Chicago.

The people wait patiently in the dark cold of the previous night to cross themselves and bid farewell to Joseph. On the first night of visitation, the priests of Chicago gather to hear Scott Donahue carry out Joseph's commission to him to preach at this service for these men for whom Joseph offers his first prayers every morning. On the second night the venerable cathedral echoes with special prayer services conducted by Jewish rabbis and by the Episcopal and Lutheran bishops. The Chicago Gay Men's Chorus sings for the man who always reaches out with understanding and support for them.

But it is the cohort of the ordinary citizens of Chicago for whom these fortunate *Friends* are surrogates this morning. Those in the pews bring their sense of loss with them so that it fills the church like bittersweet incense. They are lost themselves in their own memories when Kenneth Velo stands in the pulpit to deliver the talk that only a few months before, high above the Atlantic on their return from Rome, Joseph asks him to deliver.

He does not speak long before one feels the mood in the cathedral loosen, as darkness does, pulling its skirts away from the land at the first light of dawn. He speaks easily, conversationally, introducing himself with the designation that Joseph's mother gives him, *I'm Father Velo, the 'regular driver.'* He frames his sermon with a story of his calling as Joseph's chief assistant. *One of the greatest compliments His Eminence paid me through the years was just to fall asleep in the car. . . . He would usually fall asleep at the end of our journey. I would say, 'Cardinal, we're here. We've arrived.' . . . and the event, the ceremony, the dinner—whatever—would begin, but not before he said to me . . .* and now Kenneth slips into his pitch-perfect imitation of Joseph's voice . . . *'Our objective is to get out of here as quickly as possible.'*

And Joseph is suddenly present among his friends, whose sense of loss now lifts away completely as Kenneth recalls his

162

great achievements with the question asked by the followers of Jesus, *Didn't he teach us, didn't he show us the way?* Joseph's friends, yes, and the high priests, too, are absorbed in Kenneth's recreation of Joseph's life and his work to bring the collegial Church of Vatican Council II to full and vigorous life so that it might better serve the world. It is a journey so sweet that one wishes that Kenneth did not have to bring it to an end. But he does, very gently, recalling the night, one day less than a week before, when, with other close friends, Kenneth *viewed his casket being carried from his residence on North State Parkway—our hearts locked in pain. But as we gather this day, he comes to us as God's instrument to say, 'Peace be with you. Christ's peace I leave with you.'*

Kenneth looks out across the now peace-filled cathedral . . . *I know that there are many people watching, listening, standing with us at this hour. But I ask you to allow me just a few words with the Cardinal. You see, it has been a long, long and beautiful ride.* Kenneth looks toward Joseph's casket in the cathedral bound now into silence by grace and mystery, and speaks gently, as he does a thousand times in the car. *Cardinal. Eminence. You're home. You're home. . . .*

The stone rolls aside, the power of the Resurrection fills the cathedral as Joseph's friends surge to their feet to applaud Kenneth and, through him, Joseph whom they recognize, as the apostles do the risen Jesus, as among them again. This tide of joy runs through the remainder of the Mass and afterwards, as the choir sings the haunting Taize community hymn, *Jesus, remember me when you come into your kingdom . . .*

The Chicago Police oversee the formation of the procession, Kenneth returns to the cathedral briefly to retrieve the Cardinal's crimson biretta, places it on the dashboard of the hearse, climbs in next to the driver, and the cars begin to move, a right turn onto Chicago Avenue, then a right turn south on Michigan

Avenue, past the great crowds of people standing quietly, some waving, some weeping, across the Chicago River and then south a few more blocks before turning west into the lowering sun. The hundred cars pass through all the neighborhoods, through communities dominated by every ethnic group and every religious belief, and all along these many miles, crowds line the way, here adults and there school children, some carrying banners emblazoned with farewells to the man that they, Catholic or not, acknowledge as their Cardinal. Hundreds hold paper-cupped candles against the knife edge of November's wind in this sidewalk liturgy of thanksgiving and praise for Joseph Bernardin.

The sun is almost gone by the time that the procession reaches the Catholic cemetery that is laid out, appropriately, like the old immigrant neighborhoods, for the Polish are all buried in this quadrant, the Irish there, and the Italians just beyond. A brief prayer service is conducted in front of the tomb that immigrant Catholics built with their pennies a century ago as the final resting place for Chicago's archbishops. Hundreds of people group themselves around the tomb as the sun sets and the television floodlights illuminate the scene against the fast falling night. As the crowd sings "Amazing Grace," snow begins to drift down through the light field, snow as peaceful and gentle as Joseph himself, snow mantling everything with Joseph's gift of peace.

Cardinal. Eminence. You're home. You're home.

Joy is the flip side of trust

Perhaps the best witness I can give to priests (and other
is to be joyful — a joy based on trust and goodness

*   But being joyful does allow for sadness when there
is disunity, evil, when things are not of God

Jesus has to be my strength as I deal with
all my problems.

Morneau: I have the gift of presence. I live
in the present moment; I am really present
to people.

The quality/intensity of our joy is related to the
Lord's presence in and among us.

...neau: Read all 4 chapters of Paul's letter to the Philippi
for in it there is a call to joy, to rejoice.
Enter into dialogue with Paul. How could he
be joyful with all the problems/messiness he had
to deal with?

Who is this Lord Paul journeys with? Who empower
him to be joyful in all his afflictions?

Note the passages which strike me — then reflect
on them; pray over them. Why should I rejoice?